Images of the Soul

Daan van Kampenhout

The Workings of the Soul in Shamanic Ritual and
Family Constellations

Second Edition, 2016

Published by Carl-Auer-Systeme Verlag
und Verlagsbuchhandlung GmbH
www.carl-auer.de

Please order our catalogue:
Carl-Auer-Systeme Verlag
Vangerowstraße 14
69115 Heidelberg

Cover: WSP Design, Heidelberg
Coverpainting: "Worldcarrier" © Marleen van Engelen, 1997
Printed in Germany

Die Deutsche Bibliothek – CIP-Cataloguing-in-Publication-Data

A catalogue record for this publication is available from Die Deutsche Bibliothek.

Copyright © 2001, 2016 by Carl-Auer-Systeme Verlag und Verlagsbuchhandlung GmbH
All rights reserved. No part of this book may be reproduced by any process
whatsoever without the written permission of the copyright owner.

ISBN 3-89670-231-9

Table of Contents

Family Constellations and Shamanism ... 7
Introduction ... 11

1. Descriptions of Shamanism and Constellations ... 17
2. Paradigms of Healing ... 23
3. Family Constellations and Shamanic Rituals ... 30
4. Taking on Suffering on Behalf of Others ... 37
5. The Importance of Ancestral Strength ... 46
6. The Experience of Timelessness ... 53
7. Manifestations of the Soul and the Spirit ... 65
8. The Multiple Soul ... 74
9. The Soul, the Four Bodies, and the Personality ... 84
10. The Presence of the Dead ... 95
11. The Soul and the Constellation Process ... 103
12. Effects of Constellations ... 114
13. Development of the Soul ... 124
14. Some Pitfalls ... 135
15. Rituals ... 142

About the Author ... 156

Family Constellations and Shamanism

As Daan started to write me letters about his observations of how the family constellation mirrored many elements of shamanic experiences, I was on the one hand surprised, and on the other hand, fascinated. The basic position of reverence for powers that we cannot clearly understand; the differentiation between strength and weakness at the energetic level that enables us to understand what helps us or harms us; the meaning of space as opposed to time in the sense that the essence is visible in space, remains timeless in space, and only reveals its healing effect when it is not dulled by questions about the past or future: these are just some of the examples of similarities between the family constellation and shamanism. However, it was only through Daan's notes that I was able to understand some of the basic experiences from the family constellations. His notes made the family constellation much more clear to me in many areas, and I was able to recognize and switch off disturbing influences more easily. For example, questions that divert the energy from the actual event and from the clients, and are more theoretical curiosity rather than the solution for those concerned.

Daan's letters to me, which form the basis of this book, brought me into contact with a world view that in many ways, appears to contradict the norm. However, this is only at first glance. This world view forces us to examine observations that are normally passed on from mouth to mouth (and because they contradict the normal bodies of thought, we quickly suppress them) more closely. They include reports of how the appearance of the dead is experienced, for example, that at the time of their death, the dead contact those to whom they were particularly close. The living often have the impression that they have to do something for the dead person, so that their soul can find peace. The same applies to reports of spirit appearances, frequently the dead who have either committed a crime or been the victim of a crime. We are therefore familiar with the idea that there is another world that has an influence on the world of the living; and that, in the other direction, the living can also influence the dead, and sometimes must do this.

However, we cannot just simply accept what the shamans tell us about the good spirits that advise the living about what is good and bad, and the bad spirits that we have to pacify or ward off. Then it would appear – and I am being very daring here that many of the possibilities of making contact with special forces are connected to a specific place, a specific time, a specific landscape, a specific tradition. This means that they are not equally accessible to all people and that someone can and may make contact with the forces; these forces then display and open themselves to this person in his space. This does not mean that there are no connections between the different methods of access, or that a mutual enrichment is excluded. On the contrary, it is only when the special feature of each tradition and group is recognized that the different groups can move towards each other, exchange with one another and then return enriched to their own position.

There is something else to be considered here. The different traditions, and the experiences they are based on, belong to one common big soul that creates and controls them. The adaptation of a life form to its environment requires that something from the environment reaches out to the life form enabling this adaptation. The thing that reaches out to it sometimes requires extremes, but it is in doing this that it enables the special development. The life form and the environment are therefore drawn to each other. A force superior to both of them brings them together and facilitates a distinct form of togetherness and exchange. I call this common controlling force the big soul. It is not that I understand it, but this is the best image I can use to describe the knowing joint movement towards a special goal.

Development is possible where it is required by the movement of a superior power, and therefore become essential. This means that what is correct and essential at one point in time is later changed by other circumstances and views. This does not mean that the new views are more valid than the previous ones, but they facilitate developments that were not previously possible. Consider Descartes, who, in a vision, saw the world as one big machine. He was so fascinated by this view that he saw it as a revelation from God. Today, we know that this vision is no longer sufficient to understand the world, but look at what it led to, both wonderful things and destructive things. Although this view was insufficient, it pushed the development of the world forwards. It is not up to us – in my opinion – to judge what is better or worse about a development; on the one hand it is unavoidable, and on the other hand it is limited by suffering and a new understanding.

Through the surprising experience that the representatives for the individual family members actually feel like the people they are representing without knowing anything about them, the family constellation has opened an access to layers of the soul, many of which were previously hidden in our culture. In addition, when the representatives really remain collected, they are driven by an irresistible force into a movement, through which, hidden or forgotten experiences are brought to light. Through this movement, when the representatives submit themselves to it, solutions are found for the individuals and their family and kin. These solutions enable separated parties to re-unite, family members in conflict to forgive one another, and old wrongs to be righted. What is attributed to good helping spirits in shamanism can be described here as being brought about by a common soul.

The surprising thing is that these effects do not just come from the living, but also from the dead, who may be long forgotten. They make contact during a family constellation in the sense that they show what has to be put right, so that the living can be released from the consequences of past wrongs and the side-effects of past external fates; the living, by respecting the dead, enable them to retreat and finally find peace.

Family constellations enable us to experience what is known and determined in shamanism by images and rituals in a different way, a way that can be experienced by everybody. However, family constellations require experience and knowledge to be applied in the most useful way.

The family constellations and the shamanic rituals therefore meet each other at decisive points. Both can complement and enrich each other with their views and experiences and still retain their own special quality.

Bert Hellinger

Introduction

I got to know the family constellations in 1998 as a participant in a seminar lead by Gabrielle Borkan, and I was deeply impressed by their healing power. Intrigued and touched by the systemic work, I soon started to participate regularly in seminars lead by her and by other trainers as well. However, it was not long before I started to notice something strange: most facilitators used a peculiar sentence in their introduction of the work. Sooner or later I would hear something like: *"Through a process we do not understand,* the participants who represent family members of the clients will experience the feelings of the actual person they represent." How strange that they all said something similar! Why would the facilitators of family constellations collectively fail to understand such an essential aspect of the constellation process? For me, having many years of experience in shamanic practice, the family constellations did not seem completely mysterious. As an experiment, I started to observe the dynamics of the representation process as carefully as I could, trying to describe them as a shamanic phenomenon. Maybe, I thought, at some point I would be able to come up with some helpful answers for people who wanted to understand more about the processes involved in systemic work.

After some time I had the following dream. I was finding my way alone in a natural landscape with hills, rocks, and trees. The landscape was not made of true physical matter; I understood that I was walking around in a specific zone in the world of energy that had gotten its form from theoretical structures in mankind's thinking. I was looking for the theoretical foundation of the energetic and spiritual aspects of Bert Hellinger's systemic work. I knew that this theory would be imprinted on the landscape somewhere, or more accurately: that it would be part of the landscape in the form of a natural structure. After some time I ended up in a nice and spacious cave. Sunlight was shining through cracks and holes in the ceiling. On the wide, flat ground, I saw many flat pieces of rock. Most of them were between fifteen and thirty centimeters wide and long; all were irregularly shaped. There were various sizes, various colors, various types of stone. I knew that this collection of material represented the theory about systemic work at the particular point in time that I had the dream. I noticed that the stones on the ground were fragments of other, bigger stones. As I tried to walk on them, I was not very sure of my footing because the stones were not put together very well. They did not fit tightly together and as I walked on them some slipped away, others wobbled and bounced. In the dream, I understood that the place I had found needed some improvement. People who in their minds or dreams would come here to explore it would not find a coherent structure. It was clear that the theory about systemic work needed some improvement; an improvement in the theory would automatically result in an improved stone structure on the floor of this cave in the world of spirit. The most important thing I understood about this new structure was that it should be made out of one specific material, not out of fragments. I could see it in my mind as a big slab of stone, smooth and clear, with variations of color and structure, but still one. Then I woke up.

At the time I had this dream, I was already involved in correspondence with Bert Hellinger, who developed the family constellations. I had participated in a series of seminars he was leading, and at one of them, he had suggested certain exercises to me. Some months later, I had a transforming spiritual experience that was directly connected to Bert Hellinger's intervention, and I felt I should write to him about this. I have described this experience in chapter five, *The experience of timelessness*. After the first letter, others followed, and I started to write down some of my thoughts on how the constellation process is based on certain spiritual principles that also lie at the foundation of shamanic practice. With hindsight, the dream was the moment when I started to see that our correspondence was leading to me writing a book about the subject.

Many aspects of the family constellations have been carefully described by various people in the 'languages' of psychotherapy, psychology, and genealogy. Each of these scientific languages is based on certain assumptions about reality, and directs attention away from certain things while leading it to others: each language necessarily has its blind spots. The fact that important parts of the constellation process have remained a mystery to many people therefore does not necessarily mean that something really inexplicable is going on. It may very well be that the languages which can be used to accurately describe the hidden dynamics in families that come to light in the constellations, are simply not suited for the task of describing the energetic principles that make it possible for one person to represent another. My dream inspired me to present a coherent theory of the energetic dynamics of the constellation process in the language of shamanism, which has not been used until now to describe systemic work. This language, like any other, has its blind spots, but is specifically helpful where the nature and the movements of the soul are concerned, exactly the area where the other languages have proven to be unsuited to the task of explaining some of the constellation's dynamics.

Western scientific languages give analytical explanations. Shamanic language does not usually explain, it simply describes – which is something different. The shamanic language is used to describe not only the experiences of the senses of the physical body, but also of the soul. In traditional shamanic practice, a precise description of a spiritual experience is seen as a valid explanation in itself. A shaman or medicine man will describe all kinds of spiritual and practical experiences, and leaves it up to the listener to see the connections and structures between them. Listening to traditional shamanic practitioners, but not discussing, questioning, or analyzing, certain patterns slowly become visible to the listener, deeper structures of reality start to be felt. Being taught by shamans and medicine people is different from learning a new formula or a certain technique in school. The apprentice of the shaman is given the opportunity to listen to detailed descriptions of reality and has to draw his own conclusions.

In 1979 I had my first encounter with shamanism when I met a Native American healer in a dream. He did not resemble the popular romantic picture of Native Americans in any way – he had short gray hair, wore blue jeans and a raincoat. He used no drum, no feathers or regalia. I met him in a dark place; there was scarcely any light. He simply sat down next to me on the ground, and started singing some healing songs. After some time, he invited me to sing with him. I was too shy and too moved by the songs to be able to sing, and seeing this, he put his hands on my back for some time. After a while he said it was time for him to go, we said goodbye and I woke up. The dream came when I was sixteen years old, a period of intense distress and confusion. I knew it was a gift from an unknown reality and I did not speak to anybody about my experience. It gave me the trust and strength I needed to face my challenges, and even today I still feel the warmth of this medicine man's touch on my back and I continue to receive strength from it. Two years after this dream, I only just survived malaria, and shortly after my recovery, I had another experience with a shaman. I was sleeping, and woke up in my dream. Beside my bed stood a shaman from the Arctic, dressed in a brown leather parka. He, surprisingly, introduced himself to me as my teacher. He invited me to step out of my body and bed, which I was somehow able to do, and I was subjected to a series of tests. This teacher wanted to find out how strong I was. I don't think he could have been very impressed, but still, after that dream, I continued to have more dreams in which teachers and spirits appeared to teach me. In this way, shamanism came into my life naturally and gradually. After being taught by the spirits in my dreams for some years, by chance I met a traditional Native American who understood about the nature of the human soul and the way it can be healed when it is ill, and I was invited to travel with him. Again later, I had the privilege to be welcomed at the homes of traditional shamanic practitioners. I was present when they were leading ceremonies and doing healing. Some of them supported me in the work of speaking with and interpreting the spirits for people in need, and I have been doing this work full time since 1992. I do not see myself as a shaman or medicine man, however. I feel more comfortable defining myself as someone who is committed to the study of shamanism, something I have been doing now for about twenty years. I know that my understanding of shamanic practices will never be complete. There are many things about shamanism I have yet to understand and learn.

In this book, I look at some of the questions that have been formulated in the course of the development of Bert Hellinger's work on systemic resolutions and that have not yet been answered. How is it possible that the representatives in a constellation, knowing next to nothing about a certain family, are capable of feeling and expressing the essence of the relationships between a family's members? What actually happens at that moment? These questions are connected to 'the process we do not understand' mentioned by most facilitators who lead constellations. There are also other questions that need clarification. In constellations, not only living family members are represented, but also those who have died. That a constellation can have a healing effect on a client and even on living family members that are represented is by now a fact – but do constellations also heal the dead? Such questions, and others, deserve carefully formulated answers.

Readers should realize that my use of the shamanic language is always highly personal: it has grown out of my own personal experiences and understanding, I do not represent any specific shamanic teacher, tradition, or culture. Furthermore, it may surprise some of the readers who are familiar with contemporary western shamanism that many of my descriptions of shamanic practices (and the constellation process) are essentially technical in nature. I am influenced by the traditional shamanic teachers I have studied with, and all traditionalists I have met have proved to be true technicians. From a traditional perspective, shamanism is a science – although it is a science that studies laws of nature that are not measurable by western science which observes physical matter only.

Since the beginning of 2000, Bert Hellinger started to look at possibilities for further development of the constellations process, resulting in some changes in the roles of both the facilitator and the representatives. This exploration is called the "movements of the soul", and it is developing as a separate direction in the phenomenological-systemic work next to the family constellations. From a shamanic perspective there are some essential differences between family constellations and the movements of the soul, and this book has been written with only the family constellations in mind. At the moment, the exploration of the movements of the soul is still a very dynamic process, and according to my point of view it is too early to include conclusive observations about it in this book.

In this book, I concentrate on understanding the movements of the soul during the representation process, and I leave the description of the dynamics of entanglements in families in the hands of Bert Hellinger and other authors such as Gunthard Weber and Hunter Beaumont. Readers wishing to learn more about entanglements between family members should read their publications. I touch the theme of entanglements only occasionally, when my own experience and the shamanic language enable me to. I have not written this book with the intention of providing the reader with the complete descriptions of the constellations process and shamanic practice. My goal is more modest than that: I have aimed to use my understanding of shamanism to explore and clarify some of the energetic and spiritual aspects of the family constellations, aspects that have not been explained until now.

It is my wish that my work will help people to enhance their understanding of the dynamics that make the constellations possible, and that the images of the soul I present touch the reader in such a way that his or her own inner soul will recognize something of value in them.

I want to thank those people who have had a direct influence on this book. First of all I wish to thank Bert Hellinger, whose responses to my letters stimulated me to continue to explore the links between shamanic practice and constellations until I found myself writing a new book. Secondly, my teachers in shamanism, both in the physical and nonphysical worlds, who provided me with the opportunities to learn and let my mind and soul expand. Then I wish to thank all the facilitators who led seminars on family constellations in which I participated, and of them I especially wish to thank Gabrielle Borkan. I also want to thank Jan Jacob Stam, Peter van Zuilekom, and Otteline Lamet, whose seminars I attended during some phases of my research. Thanks to Oscar David, for not only encouraging me to write, but for simply putting me to work again and again. For many reasons I would not have written this book without him.

Daan van Kampenhout
September 2000

1. Descriptions of Shamanism and Constellations

Shamanic practice and systemic work are complex phenomenons, and many books can be – and are – written about them. Throughout my exploration of the relationship between the two, I will describe many aspects of both shamanic ritual and family constellations and the reader's understanding about the two disciplines will become progressively more vivid and clear. However, before actually starting a comparison, I want to start with two separate and short descriptions of shamanism and family constellations. In this way, I wish to provide those readers who are not familiar with one, or either of them with a starting point.

'Shamanism' is a term used in anthropology. It was originally used to describe the spiritual traditions and practices of various ethnic groups in Siberia, Mongolia, Lapland, and parts of Alaska and Canada. The traditional spiritual practice of the nomadic groups of the arctic and subarctic zones of the northern hemisphere is quite complex, and varies considerably from tribe to tribe, so here I can give only a very simplified and summarized overview. One basic shamanic concept is that the world we live in is only one of many. The different worlds are seen as segments of a vertically layered universe; they are united by an axis that runs through them, often called the world tree. Above us are the upper worlds; below us are the lower worlds. These other worlds are inhabited by spirits of all kinds. There are the great forces of nature: the four spirits of the four directions, the mountains, the seas, the thunder. There are animal spirits, plant spirits, and the souls or spirits of humans who have died. There are smaller spirits of nature, among them such entities as those who are called elves and goblins in Western Europe. According to the shamanic traditions, some of the spirits act as teachers and helpers while others are not interested in humans. Some are even occasionally violent and ill disposed towards us. The shamanic upper and lower worlds are not the same as Christian heaven and hell. In the upper worlds, you can find places of wisdom, but also places where the spirits try to deceive humans. In the lower worlds, there are many places of vitality and strength, but also regions where you can get sick, stuck, or lost. The various worlds interact with each other at all times; they overlap and merge in many ways, symbolically united by the world tree. You could see the three worlds as a number of slides projected on the same white screen at the same time. Because the lower, middle, and upper worlds are interwoven, it is possible to move from one to the next. When people have problems or suffer from disease, a shaman may go and try to find information and healing power in the other worlds. Often, when help is needed, the spirits can offer valuable support. Many spirits can see what is going on in our world, and they can share their point of view with us. Often, but not always, their information can be used to bring balance and healing. Traditionally, it is only the shaman who will attempt to speak with the spirits, and he is capable of doing so after entering a trance. He can either undertake the journey to the other worlds to go and talk with the spirits, or he may call the spirits towards him and talk with them in that way.

Classical shamanism has various characteristics that set it apart from other traditions in which people contact the spirits for healing and information. When the shaman has to speak to the spirits because a troubled individual requests his help, he traditionally dresses in a shaman costume. The traditional Siberian shaman costumes are very impressive: covered in images of spirits and animals made in leather, textile, and iron, heavily fringed with leather strips and textile ropes (called snakes), a shaman costume may weigh up to twenty or thirty kilos. Dancing in his costume, the shaman is soon exhausted and falls into a trance. As the trance deepens, the shaman sings improvised songs made up of words and the sounds of animals, and he plays a monotonous rhythm on a large flat drum. When the trance has deepened, the shaman is capable of communicating with the spirits.

In Siberia, shamanism has just barely survived the Soviet period. In the nineteen thirties, the Communist party started an organized campaign against shamans; they were seen as enemies of the state. The years under Stalin proved to be fatal: most shamans were killed, many of them in prison camps. People continued to use shamanic practices only in the remotest areas. Nowadays, following the collapse of the Soviet state, there is a shamanic revival in many parts of Siberia, especially in the southern Siberian regions. However, the link with tradition has been broken and modern Siberian shamanism is to a great extent a reconstruction in which just fragments of the past survive.

The spirituality of the indigenous tribes of North America is closely related to classical shamanism, but there are some important differences between them and the practices of peoples from more northern regions. The trances of Siberian shamans are spectacular and dynamic compared to those of Native American medicine men. Siberian shaman songs are improvised; the healing songs of North American traditions have fixed words and melodies. Finally, the North American medicine people seldom or never use shaman costumes. Still, the spiritual traditions of the Native Americans are often classified as shamanism too: their view of the spirits and their worlds, and the way to approach these, are basically identical to those of the Siberian peoples.

Today, most western people use the word shamanism to describe not a form but a *content*: it now means having a conscious relationship with the spirits. According to this new definition, the healers of the Australian Aboriginals, African diviners, Balinese trance-mediums, and many others are all shamans of one kind or another. Today, the healing practices of almost every non-western culture that lives (or lived) in close relationship with the earth is classified as shamanism by most westerners. When I refer to 'traditional shamans', I mean Siberian and Mongolian shamans and North American medicine men, so I usually stick to the older anthropological definition which includes just the spiritual practices of the northern arctic and subarctic peoples. Originally, the term shamanism described a specific *form* of communication with the spirits that included the shaman costume, improvised songs, and the great flat drums.

As with any spiritual tradition, the individual practising it determines the quality of the work. Just as some Christian priests, Jewish rabbis, and Islamic imams are great souls, while others are fairly limited in their understanding of the spiritual principles of their religion, truly great shamans practise alongside shamans who are unwise and quite incompetent. The image of shamanism has gradually reached almost mythical proportions in the western world, however. I do not share this peculiar and optimistic point of view. Shamanism is often used as a synonym for wisdom, truth, purity, non-violence, ecology, and spiritual harmony. I wish it was so, but my experience has taught me that the truth is not that simple. There may be individual shamans who embody a number of such qualities, but that does not mean that the shamanic culture as a whole embodies them too. For me, shamanism is not a dream of a golden past; it is a spiritual language. People with talent will learn it more easily than others, and their control of the language will be greater, but everyone can learn to express themselves in it to a certain extent.

The family constellations were developed by Bert Hellinger as part of his work on systemic resolutions. A constellation is a way of dealing with negative effects of disruptive events in the history of a family. It is not a form of psychotherapy. In typical psychotherapy, the roots of problems such as a negative self-image may be traced and difficult experiences of childhood or other traumatic events can get reframed. It is possible to do this because psychotherapy deals with conscious or unconscious messages somebody received as he was growing up. For example, if your mother has always told you that you are stupid, you received the message that you had little or no value. If that feeling was reinforced through further negative experiences, a poor self-image is the result. Psychotherapy may be of help here. The family constellations however are not concerned with these kind of processes. Systemic work concerns itself with family stories and events that are hardly even noticed by the personality, events, and half-secrets that somehow still influence the quality of life and the choices of the soul. Imagine a woman who has lost two or three children after the birth of her first child. Years later, her granddaughter is unable to get pregnant. A psychotherapist would not see a relation between the two facts, but in a seminar on family constellations, the facilitator would immediately be alert for a possible entanglement between the grandmother and granddaughter. The body of knowledge slowly acquired by studying many thousands of family constellations suggests that events such as the early deaths of the grandmother's children could be an important factor in the origins of the granddaughter's infertility. Unconsciously, on a soul level, the granddaughter may have taken on the fate of her grandmother. Bert Hellinger and other people using family constellations do not stand alone in such findings. There are various therapeutic and psychoanalytic schools that have discovered similar dynamics through their research, and much has been learned about how important events in a family may have negative effects on family members born two, three or even more generations later. What sets Bert Hellinger apart is the use of family constellations, the conclusions that can be drawn from them, and especially the interventions that he developed.

Constellations are done in groups, under the guidance of a facilitator. After a short interview with the client, the facilitator determines which family members are needed to set up a constellation. The client chooses the representatives for those family members from the other participants in the seminar. He invites people to represent, for example, his father, mother, sister, and two brothers. He also chooses a representative for himself. People who are asked to represent the client's family members can refuse to be a representative, but usually they are willing to be of help. The client then sets up the constellation. Without speaking, he places the various representatives one by one in the group room. When the representatives are placed, they experience distinct and precise sensations. The younger brother may feel close to his father and experience pure hatred towards his eldest brother. The sister may feel aloof; she does not feel part of the family at all. The mother may feel so tired she cannot stand anymore and literally drops down onto the floor after two minutes. Often the client who has set up the constellation is astonished by the way the representatives react. The sister was indeed always on her own, hardly interested in anyone else. Mother was always complaining and tired. The younger and elder brother hated each other, but the younger one liked his father. Such feelings of the various family members have not been discussed during the facilitator's interview with the client; on the contrary, stories about what was felt by whom, how this one judged the other – these are always omitted. Importance is only given to the actual events, not to the stories and family myths about them. Who died, and how? Who had a significant relationship or was married to whom? Who had an accident, was excluded, or had an otherwise difficult fate? During the constellation, the facilitator studies the body language and reactions of the representatives in order to understand the dynamics operating in the family. When the structure is clear, he searches for balancing or healing movements in order to find an alternative for the destructive entanglements that have become apparent. He may move some of the representatives to another place and study the various reactions to this intervention. He may ask a representative to say certain key sentences that express what is going on or what needs to be said. Such sentences are short and often have an archaic quality: "Now I see you as my father.", "I take you as my wife.", "I leave the guilt with you.", "I consent.".

Sometimes, in the course of the process, more representatives of family members have to be brought into the constellation in order to find a resolution, sometimes not. The process of finding a resolution may take less than ten minutes or more than an hour. Often a resolution is found, but not always. When there is no resolution, the reason is most likely that information about some key family members is missing. Sometimes a facilitator feels that he cannot intervene; it is as if a consciousness overshadows the family and prevents the constellation from developing. Towards the end of a constellation, the client himself may be asked to stand in his own place and so replace his own representative, but this is not always necessary. Often it is enough for the client to be a witness to the constellation and see a new harmony emerge out of old entanglements and confusion. A family constellation is a singular event; people do not set up a weekly event over a period of time as if they were some kind of therapy sessions. It may take a year or more before the effects of it are felt. Many people, but not all, have reported that after setting up their own family in a constellation, important healing shifts that are directly related to the work done in the constellation have happened; not just for themselves but also for their family members.

2. Paradigms of Healing

Shamanic rituals for healing and problem solving are based on a set of paradigms and spiritual laws, many of which lie at the foundation of the family constellations as well. However, before looking at what the constellations and shamanic rituals have in common, it is helpful to get an insight into the most important underlying principles of shamanic practice.

One of the ways to explore the basic paradigms of shamanism is to look at how shamanism relates to classical psychotherapy. Shamanism and psychotherapy both aim to heal the psyche and soul, but their points of view on how to facilitate healing are often contradictory. Because they differ in so many ways, shamanism and psychotherapy shine a very clear light on each other.

When I compare shamanism and psychotherapy, I have to simplify and polarize both of them; in this way, the differences between the two become clearer. When I mention shamanism in this comparison, I am referring to shamanism as it has been defined by older anthropological definitions: the spiritual practices of Siberian, Mongolian, and North American nomadic tribes. I use the word psychotherapy to indicate classical psychotherapy: a therapy given by a psychotherapist to people who are suffering from psychological dysfunctions, for example paranoia, neurosis, or phobias. My use of the term psychotherapy does not encompass the great variety of therapies developed for people who are basically healthy and want support for their personal development or spiritual growth. Before I start my comparison, it is important to know that classical shamanism is used not only to heal pathological psychological states, but also to diagnose and treat physical diseases. Psychotherapy is principally only used for psychological problems and obstructions. The fields of traditional shamanism and classical psychotherapy therefore only partially overlap. Today, in the new age movement and in alternative health care, many kinds of therapies and types of shamanic work are offered, including a variety of combinations of both. Remarkably, traditional shamanism and classical psychotherapy are not often used on the alternative circuit. Traditional shamanism is very rare, and it is hard to find access to it, while for many people, classical psychotherapy is out of date because it does not concern itself with the spiritual dimension of life. However, the two practices continue to be cornerstones of most of the more recently developed therapeutic schools and shamanic training. Comparing psychotherapy and shamanism in their most basic form therefore not only gives insight into the foundational paradigms about healing on which they are based, but into more recent therapeutic approaches and shamanic work as well.

The first difference between shamanism and psychotherapy can be seen when you look at the construction of the context considered essential for healing. Essentially, the difference can be summarized as follows: the therapeutic process develops along a time line whereas shamanism builds a structure in space. Let us first consider the psychotherapeutic approach. When you go and see a therapist for counseling, the therapist will propose a period of time in which the work will be done. If you are phobic and start seeing a therapist in March, the psychotherapist will be able to sketch a structure of the therapy through time: after the initial research, he will be able to trace and uncover the roots of your fear in April or May; by June, you should be able to make some steps directly related to solving the fear; in August, you should be able to see substantial improvement. Finally, by November, you should be able to function well enough to stop the therapy. Even though this process might take longer or shorter than planned, and different therapists have different opinions about its duration, the therapeutic process is always seen and described as a gradual development over a period of time. Shamanic healing is placed in a very different context. Although the duration of the preparations for a shamanic ritual and the ritual itself can of course be measured in hours, days or even weeks, the actual shamanic healing is a not gradual process that develops over time. Shamanic healing takes place in a timeless zone, a mythical time in which all that ever was and ever will be is present. During a shamanic ritual, everything is aimed at disconnecting the participants from a linear experience of time, something that is explored in detail in a later chapter, *The experience of timelessness*. The shaman focuses his attention on the experience of space, not of time. The four directions in the four corners, the sky and the upper worlds above, the earth and the lower worlds below: these are the primary anchor points for the healing, not the months of April, August, and November. Healing takes place in a sacred space, the structure of which is made visible through altars and images. All the people who witness the ritual participate in a timeless drama in which all healing power – in fact all that exists – is present. During the ritual, the shaman invites the specific powers that can contribute to the healing with prayers and offerings of food, water, and smoke that are placed on altars. An altar is seen as an anchor that links both visible and invisible worlds; it serves as the embodiment of the invited healing power. There is no 'symbol' here; there is no separation between object and subject. In the course of the ritual, an altar dedicated to a particular spirit becomes that spirit. Shaman, client, and spectators are surrounded by the spirits. All spiritual powers are given their own place in this ritual reconstruction of the spiritual universe. Just as all the cosmic powers have their own place, so too, according to the shamanic traditions, have the powers and energies within the body and psyche of the client. When a power or energy is in its rightful place, it has a beneficial effect; when it is displaced it creates disturbance. Entering the mythical timeless space of the shamanic ritual, a shaman can retrieve a lost part of the soul and bring it home; he can take foreign energy out of the client's body and return it to where it came from. When all the energies are back in the places where they belong, the result is health and things in life will start to organize themselves in better ways.

Structuring the healing within a timeframe or within a spatial structure is the first and maybe the most fundamental difference between a therapeutic process and shamanic healing, and it has far reaching consequences. The effect of the paradigm that healing happens through an organization of space allows for example, that shamanic healing may happen in a remarkably short time. In shamanic healing, time is simply not a relevant factor. An individual may be terribly ill or completely confused when the ritual starts, and be in perfect health just hours later. I met a woman who threw up a stomach tumor as big as an egg straight after an all-night healing ceremony; the surgery that was scheduled to take place in the hospital was cancelled because the tumor was already gone. I have witnessed more similar events. From the shamanic point of view this is logical and not miraculous. When somebody needs healing, the physical space in which the healing takes place is transformed through prayer and the placing of altars. The space becomes a mini-cosmos in which all necessary spiritual powers are potentially present and can be addressed. The shaman chooses which spirits will be asked to work on the client. The client may be asked to move from altar to altar to be presented to the spirits, but often the client is directed to one specific place and stays there for the duration of the ceremony. While the client remains stationary, the shaman organizes the ritual by manipulating the forces within the space. He may, for example, in the course of the ritual, move from altar to altar or flag to flag, asking the forces of the four directions to enter the room and contribute to the healing. When the ritual ends, the altars are dismantled and the experience of linear time returns. The client emerges from the ritual and is not the same as he was before; he is touched by the spirits and through that touch he is changed. The powers of creation have recreated his life in the most literal sense. Sometimes it may take hours, days, or weeks in order for the healing to fully integrate into all aspects of the client's life, but when the ceremony is over, healing is done. If it was successful, the problem is solved, and if it was not successful, the ceremony is usually not repeated, since the spirits have already done what they were able to do. There is no gradual development of a healing strength as in a therapeutic process; in shamanism healing is a singular event, sudden and direct.

A second difference between shamanism and psychotherapy becomes clear when the roles of the shaman and the therapist are studied. The shaman is the expert who knows his way through the healing structures of the universe and is able to activate those powers that are needed in a certain situation. Having done this, his work is basically finished: in a way, he retreats. The responsibility for the ritual is in hands of the shaman, but the responsibility for the healing is in the hands of the spirits. The activities of the shaman during the ritual principally serve to keep the structure of the mythical space intact, his songs are sung to support spirits doing the healing work. A shaman may also do healing work himself, but even then he usually follows the orders and suggestions of the spirits. A psychotherapist is much more involved in the actual healing process; he has taken charge of it. Therapists make suggestions, invent solutions, and give clients homework. The therapist has to confront the client with inconsistencies in his life story, evaluate the client's experience of reality, and direct the attention towards issues that the client is avoiding. A psychotherapist actively directs the process and makes choices about the way the therapy evolves.

Up until now, we have seen that the psychotherapist's client signs up for a number of meetings over a period of several months, and during that time he is guided by the therapist. A shaman's client enters a timeless space in which the shaman makes the structure of the spiritual universe visible. The spirits are called in, and they are in control of the actual healing while the shaman is in control of the ceremony.

A shaman mobilizes forces and powers from the outside: healing spirits and forces of nature. A therapist however, tries to activate the qualities that are dormant within the client. This signifies another important difference between the two disciplines. The psychotherapeutic schools assume that there is a potential within the client himself that can be used to facilitate healing, so therapists help their clients to develop new psychological and social skills. During a therapeutic process, a client learns to see himself and his story in a different light and will start to practise new ways of behavior. The skills he acquires may already be operative in some aspects of his life or they may be completely newly developed tools. It makes an enormous difference whether you see a client as a person who can develop his personality from within because it is full of potential, or, within the context of healing, you see a client as a static field that can only change when he absorbs and integrates energy and power from the outside. A therapist relies on the strength and potential of the client, even if the necessary qualities are completely covered up and practically invisible at the moment the therapy starts. A shaman relies on strength from the outside, the spirits; on external rather than internal intelligence.

Another important difference between shamanic healing and psychotherapy is that shamanic healing is not just organized to help a single client. In fact, when a shamanic healing is organized, everybody is welcome. The more people present, the better. Family, friends, neighbors, the doors are open for everybody. The shaman himself does not arrive on his own either; he may bring one or more assistants, some singers and drummers, his partner, children, and other relatives. In a therapeutic setting, there are just the therapist and his client, nobody else. A psychotherapist may recognize that a client became ill because of stress and disease that originates in the family, but psychotherapy still aims to help just one person. In a shamanic context, when a single person is ill, the whole family system and community are thought to be in need of healing, and it would be useless to welcome just the client for the healing ceremony. The whole community needs to be present so that everybody can be healed, and therefore everybody is welcome to show up and participate. During the healing ritual, each person prays for the client but also for his or her own pain and troubles, and it often happens that several people are touched by the spirits and find healing of one kind or another.

A last important difference between shamanic ritual healing and psychotherapy can be seen when you look at the difference in availability of treatment. In the Western world, it is fairly simple to find a therapist nowadays. If you want therapy today, you can have it tomorrow. Even people who do not have enough money to pay a therapist can often get some kind of psychotherapy, since various therapies are covered by health insurance. Shamanic ritual healing is much harder to organize, not just for people in the Western world but also for those who live in traditional shamanic cultures. First, you have to find a medicine man or shaman that is known to be able to deal with your specific illness or problem. Next, you have to approach him; usually that means you bring certain traditional gifts as you ask for a healing ceremony. The shaman may not answer you immediately, he may take some days to 'look into it', waiting for a dream or a reaction from the spirits. He may agree to a healing ritual or not, and only when the answer is 'yes' will a date be set. You need to make preparations, prepare the various altars according to the detailed instructions of the medicine man or shaman. It will probably take a lot of effort, time, and even money to collect the material and make the altars. You have to prepare the space in which the ritual will be held. You have to prepare a feast that is held for all participants after the ritual; that means you have to buy lots of food and get people to cook it. You have to buy or make gifts for all who help you. A shamanic healing ritual is only possible when many people contribute their time, energy, and money. In fact, all these preparations have a practical reason. Only when you are really prepared to go through all the preparations will you ask for a shamanic healing, and that means that when the ritual finally happens, the shaman finds a client who is really committed. The paradox is that although a shamanic healing ritual costs a lot of money in this way, the shaman himself is not paid. The sponsor of the ritual, the patient or one of his family members, is supposed to make the shaman a gift, but that is all. In traditional shamanic society, the gifts for the shaman are practical and valuable. This principle of not paying should however not be confused with just giving something of little or no value. In small and closed communities, the people know each other's needs precisely, and so if a shaman's fishing nets are old and broken, he would receive a new net from a thankful client; if a medicine man's blankets are thin and torn, he would receive a new blanket. Psychotherapy works the other way around. You need nobody to help you prepare, you can get therapy easily, and the money it costs you goes directly to the therapist.

There are many other differences between the traditional shamanic and classical psychotherapeutic disciplines; for example, the way therapists and shamans are trained. A therapist has voluntarily chosen to become a therapist but a traditional shaman has no choice; he is taken by the spirits for the job. In shamanic cultures, people only start training to become a shaman because the spirits want this. If you are chosen, the traditions say the cost of refusing to become a shaman is very high: severe illness, madness, or even suicide. However, no matter how interesting it would be to continue comparing shamanism and psychotherapy, I only wanted to define shamanism just so far as would be helpful to start to explore its relation with family constellations. Having reached this point, it is time to move on to the next chapter.

3. Family Constellations and Shamanic Rituals

Bert Hellinger's systemic work contains both shamanic and psychotherapeutic elements. When the facilitator interviews the client and when, during or after the constellation, he confronts him or guides him to a new understanding, the interventions sometimes come straight from the handbooks of psychotherapy. It even happens regularly that during the interview with the client, a facilitator only makes some therapeutic interventions and does not let a client set up a constellation at all; sometimes psychotherapy is a more effective tool for healing or insight than a constellation. The dynamics of the actual family constellations are however closely related to shamanism, because shamanic healing rituals and constellations are partly based on the same energetic and spiritual principles. In order to get a clear view of the common ground between family constellations and shamanism, I will return, one by one, to the various polarities described in the previous chapter. Summarized, the polarities are:

Psychotherapy	*Shamanism*
1. Healing on a time line	Healing through organization of space
2. Gradual development	Sudden change
3. Therapist directs actual healing process	Spirits are in charge of the healing
4. Healing strength from the inside	Power from outside sources
5. Healing of the individual	Healing of the community
6. Easy access	Many preparations
7. The therapist is paid in money	The shaman receives a gift

Looking at the first polarity, time versus place, it is obvious that the constellations are based on an orientation in space. During a constellation, just like in shamanic rituals, the boundaries between past, present, and future are dissolved. The dead are represented next to the living and in this way they are alive and speak. Former partners are present, lost children are found and held. Constellations are possible only when linear time is left behind. During a constellation, the healing process is made possible through shifts and movements of the representatives within the actual space of the constellation; representatives are moved around until all have found a place in which they feel strong and balanced. In the constellations, it can be observed that the feelings of any given representative may change considerably as soon as just one or two other representatives are moved by the facilitator from one place to another. When one or two representatives have changed place, the whole field has changed and from a certain perspective, all the representatives are in a new position. Through careful manipulation of representatives in the space, healing is facilitated for all. With regard to the polarity time versus place, the constellations are firmly positioned on the side of shamanic ritual.

The next polarity is the gradual development over the months during psychotherapy versus the sudden change of a single shamanic healing. Just like a shamanic ritual, each constellation is a singular event. There are no series of constellations, while in therapy, one would attend weekly sessions. Although some clients do set up several constellations in a certain longer period of time, each constellation remains a single event. After a constellation is held, there is no evaluation, no follow-up. There is no gradual healing process; the constellation facilitates a healing movement which is sudden and concrete. On the spiritual level, what remains is a shift in the energy of the soul; on the personality level, the result are images: images of the various phases of the constellation, and especially of how it looked just before it was ended. These images are remembered and can change something in the client, and in the time after the constellation, the effect of this change slowly becomes clear. All of these are the characteristics of shamanic healing rituals too. A client leaves a healing ritual with the clear sense that something has shifted, and without any effort on his part except continuing to memorize the feeling he had when the ritual ended; the effects of this change become apparent in the time after the ritual.

Seen from the third set of principles, the therapist's active guidance of the actual healing process versus the passive support of the shaman, the facilitator of a constellation takes up and mixes both the roles of the shaman and the psychotherapist. All the time, the facilitator reacts to the body language of the representatives and the information they provide. There are moments when a facilitator actively guides and steers the constellation and is in control of the process. There are also periods of time when he retreats and lets the constellation take its own course for a while, only to intervene when a healing movement gets stuck. Both an active and passive approach are combined.

With regard to the polarity of inner potential versus power from the outside, it is clear that in family constellations the actual healing power comes from outside, seen from the position of the client. In constellations, the energy is carried by the representatives; the client himself merely sits at the side and watches the constellation unfold. Only at the end might a client take his own place in the constellation to absorb the generated power and the new structure of his family's field. Power from the outside is literally brought in when a representative feels weak and has no access to strength: the facilitator will then typically bring in some additional representatives, for example parents, grandparents, or other ancestors who carry strength.

Examining the fifth polarity, healing of the individual versus healing of the community, the constellations once more are closer to shamanism than to psychotherapy. In a constellation, a resolution is sought that touches many who are represented, not just the client. In fact, it would even be impossible to help just the client, since the problems addressed in constellations originate in the totality of the represented system. A true resolution necessarily relieves all those who are part of the constellation. During a constellation, a single client is the focus point, but the same is the case during a shamanic healing ritual. The client's need for healing is necessary to direct the development of a constellation and keeps all movements connected to a central anchor.

Looking at polarities six and seven, systemic work should be placed on the side of psychotherapy. Family constellations are relatively easily available. Someone interested in setting up a family constellation can simply check which seminars are available; he can choose one he would like to participate in and pay a certain amount of money as he registers. No further preparations are needed.

There are other characteristics of the constellations that could be classified as shamanic, characteristics that have not been mentioned in the comparison between shamanism and psychotherapy. For example, with regard to the issue of spirits, shamanic rituals and family constellations are quite close to each other. According to my personal experience, spirits are sometimes present during family constellations, specifically the souls of dead people. I do not mean that dead family members are represented by living people; I have sometimes seen the disembodied souls of dead people in the room where a constellation was set up. Sometimes the dead will stand within the actual constellation; sometimes they just stand at the edge. The dead are only seldom present during psychotherapy; that type of work simply does not draw them in so often. During regular psychotherapy, the client may address issues concerning those who have died. He will work with his inner images of the dead and process his grief and anger – but there usually is no recognition of the fact that the dead themselves may still be around in one way or another. During constellations however, the dead sometimes show up spontaneously. I will continue to explore the issue of the presence of the dead in constellations in various other chapters; here I just want to mention this phenomenon.

There are also other spirits than the souls of the dead that can be invited in rituals or constellations. In systemic work, representatives sometimes embody abstract forces. Such an abstraction may still be within familiar human dimensions when it concerns a 'future lover' or an 'unknown victim', but what do we think of people representing death, poverty, France, the future, or Judaism? These, to name just a few, can also be represented in a constellation. According to shamanic traditions, everything that we know exists both in this physical world and in the world of spirit. Plants, animals, rocks, rivers – all of these have souls or spirits, and so do quite a lot of abstract forces and concepts. When such a force or concept is represented in a constellation, that power can no longer be considered as an abstraction. It now has a face, a name, a warm body, eyes that can be looked into. The representative experiences the essence of that abstraction in his thoughts, feelings and physical sensations. There is no symbol anymore; abstraction has turned into concrete experience. I have represented death on several occasions during systemic work, and that experience was sometimes completely physical and very intense. Once I embraced a man who was terminally ill, preparing for death. Responding to the invitation of my open arms, he slowly moved forward to let himself be embraced by me. He and I moved as if we were in slow motion. The sensation I had when he accepted my invitation and surrendered was extraordinarily intimate. An overwhelming but still very subtle wave of energy washed from him to me, and we became one; I could literally experience no more boundaries between us. Representing death, I experienced myself as a limitless energy, and surprisingly I felt more physical and alive then ever. I have never felt this particular sensation before or since this constellation; apparently it was only possible to feel it as a representative of death. Other people who have represented archaic powers in constellations have had similar powerful and very distinct experiences. The constellations confirm in this way what the shamanic traditions say; abstractions can manifest as living entities. In the context of the constellations, representatives are their hosts; the body and mind of the representative serve as their temporary body and mind.

The use of language during constellations has an archaic quality to it, similar to the use of language in shamanic context. Instead of habitual conversation, during shamanic practice there are just prayers and invocations. Sometimes, to break the tension that is the result of prolonged concentration, a shaman may make some jokes so that everybody laughs for a moment. Then the prayers are resumed. Some shamanic traditions even make use of special languages during the ceremony, called 'shaman's language'. During constellations, the representatives also refrain from using language in the normal daily way. The healing movements suggested by the facilitator are strengthened by sentences that the facilitator suggests. These sentences are not the type of sentences that are used to tell a story; they express a timeless and archaic quality. A father who was never able to accept his child opens his eyes and is asked to say: "Now I see you as my child". A man who wronged his sibling and suddenly sees the effect of what he did says: "Now I see your pain." A dying woman is finally able to give up her inner struggle to accept her fate and can tell death: "I consent." Spoken within the context of the constellation, these sentences can carry an extraordinary emotional and spiritual charge and deeply move all those who are present. In the same way, the simple prayers during a shamanic ritual sometimes seem to electrify the air and touch the heart of all those present. Both in shamanism and constellations, language is not used to explain, but to heal.

The presence of souls of those who have passed on, representation of abstract forces and archaic use of language, all these are characteristics that shamanic rituals share with the constellations. But next to these shared traits, some essential differences between traditional shamanism and family constellations can also be observed.

One very important difference between the two is that according to the shamanic traditions, people need to purify themselves before and after they have been in contact with spirits, especially where the souls of the dead are concerned. All those present during a ritual are touched with the smoke of a smoldering mixture of herbs with purifying qualities, sprinkled with water, fanned with feathers, or spiritually purified by other means. This kind of purification is a standard procedure. Firstly, purification is needed to cleanse the mind and energy of daily concerns. After purification, communication with the spirits becomes easier and there is less chance of incorrectly interpreting what they have to say. Beside this practical fact, we should remember that the spirits come from another world. As they enter a ritual – or a constellation – people may involuntarily pick up something that the spirits brought with them. Just as someone who walks into our home may stain the carpet because his shoes are dirty, so the spirits may accidentally bring in something that is not welcome. When the spirits are contacted, a spiritual purification is a sensible hygiene precaution. Spiritual purification also has a psychological function; it is good to consciously separate from the spirits after being in contact with them. If people, after a ceremony, do not direct their attention firmly to the physical world, the spirits might continue to affect them. In systemic work, purification techniques are used neither before nor after a constellation, and in general, very little attention is given to the process of separation between the representative and the person or energy that he represents. Typically, the facilitator just says 'get out of your roles', and that is it.

Another fundamental difference between shamanic rituals and family constellations is connected to the practical organization of the space. Shamanic ritual is based on a known and static map, projected onto the space by placing various altars. During constellations, the organization of the space is not static but dynamic. Representatives are set up by the client in whatever way feels right; as long as he is concentrated and centered when he places the representatives, all the positions he chooses for them are fine. The facilitator then studies this field and attempts to harmonize it. To do this, he may use certain of the known principles that have been discovered during the development of the constellations. For example, he may remember that usually the representatives of a group of siblings feel best when they are placed in the order in which they were born: the oldest first, second one at the first's left side, the third at the left of the second, the youngest finally to the third's left side. However, although some structures of placing people in relation to each other are known, the constellation as a whole is a dynamic field that is in motion. There is no such freedom in shamanic ritual because it is based on a fixed structure. The four directions are four anchors on which certain powers are placed. These will always be in the same place and cannot move in relation to each other; the east will always be placed in the east, never in the north, south, or west. The upper world is above, the lower world below, they cannot move. Shamanic rituals are built on an old map that cannot be changed.

There are two other relevant themes that should be mentioned in this comparison between systemic work and shamanism, but since they deserve a more detailed description, each will be covered in a separate chapter. In chapter four I will explore the practice of taking on others' suffering in order to help them – which is done in both shamanic rituals and in family constellations – and chapter five deals with the importance of ancestral strength.

4. Taking on Suffering on Behalf of Others

When someone is ill or is in serious trouble, a shaman will check whether spiritual help can be given. If this is the case, he will perform a ceremony. Often he will leave the actual healing job to the spirits, but it is also possible that the shaman himself will do the healing, using the spiritual technology or science of his tradition. There are different types of shamanic healing methods, to be used in different circumstances. With the help of certain healing techniques, a shaman can remove specific illnesses; other techniques are used to harmonize the energies that run through the patient's body; again other techniques enable the shaman to bring in strength that will have a positive effect on the body and mind of the client. According to the shamanic traditions, it is not just a shaman who is able to help someone in need. Other people can give spiritual support too, in a variety of ways. Among these, there is one specific kind of spiritual help that can be given by everyone: participating in specific rituals in which it is possible to take on physical suffering on behalf of someone else. Consciously taking up suffering and dedicating this suffering to someone else's health can give a powerful impulse for healing. All the various shamanic traditions have developed and refined rituals in which people suffer on behalf of others, but those of the North American Indian cultures are best known and described, for example the peyote meeting, the sundance, and the stone people lodge or sweat lodge.

A peyote meeting is organized when an individual needs healing from the powers of the spirit world. The one who needs help has to sponsor the meeting, which practically means that he has to take care (with the help of family and close friends) of the many preparations that are needed to make the ceremony possible. Some time before the ceremony is held, the word is spread that a meeting is to be held and people are invited to attend. Under the guidance of the road man, who is the leader of the ceremony, people sing and pray from sunset till dawn. In winter, that can be a stretch of up to fourteen or fifteen hours. Starting when darkness descends is an expression of the participants' willingness to enter the darkness that is the result of the suffering of the one who needs healing. As the participants in the ceremony sit motionless through the night, singing and praying, they symbolically move from the onset of darkness, signifying the start of the problem, till it gets light – the moment when relief is found and healing is accomplished. After entering the teepee in which the meeting is held, participants do not leave their place until the ceremony is over. Each participant is a witness to the suffering of the one who asked for the ceremony, and symbolically suffers with him as prayers for healing and resolution are spoken continuously. The songs and prayers are unified by chewing small quantities of powdered peyote, a cactus known for its consciousness-altering properties. This substance is not taken to get high, but enables the participants to enter a state in which their minds and intentions become one and gain strength. The peyote is known as a very powerful healing spirit, and through this spirit the individual prayers of the participants are unified. The actual healing is left to the spirit of the peyote, while the participants sit and pray. As perception of linear time fades away, the night, which is normally experienced as a period of time, actually starts to feel like a path from darkness to light, from suffering to wellbeing. Through the songs and prayers that path is strengthened and spiritually purified. In the peyote meeting, suffering on behalf of others has a refined and even partly symbolic character.

Of all rituals in which people take on suffering for others, the sundance probably takes voluntary physical suffering to the very limit. For four days, sundancers dance together around a tree that symbolizes the tree of life, and pray continuously for health and healing for their community. None of the dancers eat, and most dancers do not even drink for four days and nights; under normal circumstances this would mean a serious risk of damage to the kidneys and other organs. Sundancers not only just stop drinking; they also participate in sweat lodge ceremonies once or twice a day and lose a lot of extra water this way. However, at the end of the dance they are in good health. On the fourth day, the skin of the chest of the dancers is pierced with two hooks and these hooks are tied to the tree with leather thongs. Dancing, the dancers break themselves loose from the tree and the hooks tear through their skin. At the end, many people visit the dance; they line up and let themselves be touched by the dancers. The dancers, who by then are in a complete other state of consciousness, channel a strong healing power to the community. Through the dancers' voluntary extreme suffering, the community as a whole finds healing.

Disciplines of fasting and other kinds of deprivation are part of most, if not all, spiritual schools, varying from mild and symbolic activities to extreme and even potentially life-threatening practices. In a spiritual or religious context, physical suffering is experienced as a spiritual purification. There may be a very simple reason for this, which is not of a spiritual but rather of a psychological nature. As an individual is growing up, he has to learn the difference between what is 'good' and 'bad'. When a child has been behaving badly, it is guilty of breaking the rules and it gets punished. After the punishment, the balance is restored, the child feels free again. In essence, punishment becomes synonymous with redemption of guilt, and redemption of guilt becomes only possible through punishment. This deep psychological imprint is part of every individual's psyche. It is probably the most important reason why suffering and self-torture are experienced as purifying acts and are especially satisfying for people who are chronically ill at ease with themselves because they judge their own 'lower' impulses as evil. The mechanism installed in early childhood must also influence the form of shamanic rituals to a certain extent, but in the case of the rituals mentioned, there is more to it than just this. It makes a big difference whether suffering is taken on to purify oneself of a sense of personal guilt or whether it is done to help someone else, as it is done in shamanic rituals. The participant in a shamanic ritual has no need to redeem himself; he only suffers because somebody else needs healing. People join the ritual voluntarily in order to carry the ordeal of one individual together, and generate strength this way.

The 'stone people lodge' or sweat lodge ceremony is the most accessible of all rituals in which people can take up suffering for others who need help. The lodge is a small round hut, resembling a half ball that is placed on the earth on its flat side. This hut is usually about two and a half or three meters wide and about one and a half meters high. It is constructed by bending thin willows into a frame, and this frame will last a few years. When a ceremony is planned, the willow frame is covered with thick layers of blankets so the inside is pitch black. Participants enter; naked or clothed in very thin cotton shorts or dresses. Before the door closes at the start of the actual ceremony, glowing red-hot stones are placed in a shallow pit in the center. During the ceremony, which easily takes up two hours or more, the door will usually open three times, marking the end of a part of the ceremony. Each part of the ceremony is dedicated to a certain spirit, or to an aspect of the purification and healing process. Each time the door is opened, more hot stones are brought in. For about two hours, the participants pray together for the wellbeing of others, sitting in darkness in suffocating heat and steam. As the ceremony continues and it gets hotter and hotter, people pray harder and harder. A lodge that is dedicated specially to the healing of a single individual is usually extra hot, and all the participants pray together to ask help for this one person, guided by a medicine man. Often, towards the end of such a healing ceremony, many of the participants are so worn out that they cannot sit up straight anymore, they have to lie down as the ceremony continues. Still, the prayers continue until the medicine man or leader of the ritual ceremony indicates the work is done.

In the first stages of ritualistic self-inflicted suffering, pain and discomfort gradually build up and make the mind alert. Thinking becomes sharp and focused, the attention is drawn into the here and now. After some time, as the suffering becomes truly intense, a threshold is reached. The one who suffers can go one of two ways now: he can identify with the acute discomfort, or he can shift his attention inwards, to his own soul. In the first case, the ritual becomes an ordeal and thinking will soon become confused and associative: the pain and stress will start to lead the mind. In the second case, the mind maintains and refines its clarity as the soul takes control over the situation. This state should not be seen as dissociation because awareness of the body is still there and the suffering continues to be painfully real. The mind is simply focused on prayers, which gain more and more strength as the ceremony continues. During most of the ritual, there is continuous singing and drumming, which helps to maintain a trance that makes it relatively easy to keep the attention focussed.

The results of rituals in which suffering is taken on can vary enormously. Sometimes there are spectacular effects, sometimes there are none at all. Once I was leading a short series of purification ceremonies for a group of people, and on the second day, we did a sweat lodge dedicated to healing. Every participant went in to pray for someone else who needed help, a family member or a good friend. The host of the ceremony, who had built the sweat lodge we could use, went in the lodge for her ex-husband and daughter who had not been in contact with each other for some years. In her prayers, she was careful not to choose sides with either one of them, but continued to ask for an opening so they could speak again and resolve the troubles of the past. After the ceremony we were all having a meal in the garden and the phone rang; it was the daughter of our host. She called her mother to tell her that she had just made an appointment with her father. She knew nothing about the ceremony or her mother's prayers, but straight after we had come out of the lodge she had felt a sudden inner resolution and strength that enabled her to call her father.

Some factors that determine the outcome of a healing ritual may always remain hidden for the conscious mind. Illness and suffering may serve a hidden purpose and often are the end results of a long and complex process. Through prayers, people can offer a wish for healing, but they cannot give orders. Prayers are simply a knock on the door, asking for attention from spiritual powers that may be able to help. It is not begging, but an offering of an image of health to the spirits, asking their support so this image may become reality. After a shamanic healing ceremony, the matter should be left to rest and no further questions asked. The client's case is now in the hands of something greater, the people have done what is permitted and can do nothing more. After the ceremony, everybody, including the client, should let go and relax. If healing comes, that is very good. If not, it will be accepted.

However, there are also some factors we can name and understand that have a clear influence on the result of rituals that include suffering. For example, it is necessary that the client wants to be healed. Someone who consciously or unconsciously does not want to change will do his best to maintain the status quo no matter how much help is offered. With regard to the volunteer who takes on suffering, there are two factors that have a direct influence on the result. First, the nature of the reason that motivates him to take on suffering, and second, the ability to be conscious of the fact that the one who needs help and he himself are two different people, each leading separate lives. Sometimes it is hard to differentiate between these two factors, but by looking carefully, they can be distinguished from each other.

People take on suffering for various motives. When someone truly cares for someone and wishes him well, and as long as awareness is maintained that the other and he himself should both lead their own lives, then a ritual of suffering can be used as a powerful support. In such circumstances, the step to take on suffering is made with awareness and strength, without pretensions. However, it may also be the case that someone wants to participate in a ceremony because he does not have the strength to look at the suffering of someone he loves. His own health and good luck may feel like a burden to him, and taking on suffering will then feel like a relief. Suffering for these reasons has little to offer, it is only a form of escapism and it cannot add true strength to a ritual. Suffering can only bring power to a healing when it is given from a position of strength, not out of weakness. In the first case, when someone maintains the awareness of himself as a separate person from the ill one, he stands next to the other person. He will not try to truly stand in the other's place, he simply wishes to be near so he can give support. He wants to help carry the burden, but after doing this for a while during the ritual, his attention naturally shifts back to the responsibilities of his own life. In the second case, the one who takes on suffering actually identifies with the position of the one who needs help, and in a strange way, claims the other's suffering as his own. Seen from a certain perspective, he even pushes the person who needs help out of his rightful place; the sick one is denied his own fate, hard as that fate might be. Both individuals involved lose their individual strength in this way; this type of merging makes the situation unclear. When coming from a position of strength, voluntary suffering can transfer strength to a client. When coming from entanglements and escapism, voluntary suffering takes strength away.

Western society offers no rituals in which people suffer on behalf someone else, but people do it unconsciously all the time. In almost all cases, the result is more chaos and disease instead of healing. Recently, I worked with a mother whose daughter was a prostitute. The mother had been a prostitute too, but that was some years ago. She wanted to help her daughter to step out of the hard life she herself had left behind, and was suffering terribly from the fact that she was unable to reach the girl. The mother tried very hard to get close to her daughter, but the more she tried, the more her daughter rejected her. It was a classical example of unconscious taking on of suffering in order to help another. First, the mother had stood in the position of the prostitute, and hated it. She did not want her daughter to know too much of the difficulties she faced. The daughter, wanting to be close to her mother and even help her, found that her mother kept a certain distance, and the girl experienced this as rejection. Unconsciously she moved into prostitution, because only there she felt she could be close to her mother. By the time the girl had actually become a prostitute however, the mother had managed to start another life, and to her horror, saw where her daughter had ended up. The mother now wanted to help her daughter. Desperate because her daughter rejected her in her attempts to get close, she was at risk of being unconsciously drawn back to prostitution, the very place she had once been standing, because she felt she needed to be close to her daughter in order to help her. The daughter of course pushed her mother violently away, since allowing her near could have the consequence that her mother would be at risk of returning to the prostitution she had left behind. The boundaries between their lives were growing progressively unclear, and the dynamics of taking on each other's suffering were completely unconscious. I suggested to the mother that she should do a simple ritual. I asked her to visualize her daughter standing in front of her, and speak to her soul. I asked her to say from her own soul: "I stopped, I left that place. You can also leave. You are free now, you don't have to do this for me." The mother later told me that three days after this simple ritual, her daughter made the decision to stop being a prostitute, and stepped out. In this case, only a very basic intervention was needed to break a pattern of unconscious and destructive shared suffering.

Taking on suffering on behalf of someone else is unhealthy when it happens as a result of unconscious motives. However, when it is done with awareness and in a clear context, it may truly be of great help. Then, suffering is like helping someone who is drowning out of the water, or like clearing a path for somebody who is stuck. When someone is drowning, you jump in the water and pull him out. You have to get into the water yourself and get wet; otherwise you cannot reach him. Only later, when everything has calmed down, can you start to teach him how to swim; it is useless to try to tell him how to swim as he is panicking or dying in the water. In much the same way, when someone is going through intense suffering, it is very hard to reach him because he is identifying with his pain. In order to reach someone who is suffering, you can take on suffering yourself; in this way you stand next to them. Then, maintaining a clear mind through prayer, you do not identify yourself with the sensory experience of suffering. Your clarity of mind will affect the other person, and his identification with the suffering will lessen. When the ritual stops, you leave the place of suffering, and the other person can pull himself out too because of the connection between the two of you. Many types of shamanic healing are made possible by manipulating the positions of people and powers in a spiritualized space, which I mentioned in earlier chapters. In the description I just gave, this process can be recognized too: someone suffers, another person symbolically stands next to him; they are connected and united in suffering. When the volunteer leaves, the one who was originally suffering also has an opportunity to step out of the place of suffering. Suffering for someone else can also be understood through the metaphor of clearing a path for someone, when a similar dynamic is in operation. Sometimes someone cannot step over an obstacle in his path because of simple lack of strength. As long as he stands there, facing his difficulties, he cannot move or develop further. Most importantly, just standing there he cannot gain new strength. When somebody else joins his feeble attempts to clear the obstacle and in this way add strength, the obstacle may be cleared and the path can open up again. Then, the one who was stuck can move forward again and with some luck, he will find new strength and new opportunities. The case I mentioned first, in which a daughter found strength to call her father after her mother had suffered for both of them in the sweat lodge, is a good example of clearing a barrier for someone who was too weak to clear it on their own. The mother joined the daughter's suffering and added strength through her prayers. The daughter was able to take the strength that was offered and could move forwards again. The example also shows that this kind of help can be no more than an opportunity: the path may be cleared but it is still up to the daughter to act with wisdom and avoid repeating earlier mistakes.

There are also rituals in which people suffer for others that result in healing while none of the two dynamics of pulling someone out or breaking down an obstruction is operating. Healing is then the result of direct intervention from the spirits, and in that case it is usually not possible to describe the workings of the dynamics involved in the healing process. Recently, I was leading a healing lodge and one woman went in for her brother who had been suffering from painful eczema on his hands for many years. A few days after the ceremony, the brother's hands were clean. What precisely happened to cause this healing remains a mystery. From the shamanic point of view, all you can say is that the spirits simply took away the symptoms, maybe even the disease itself. Sometimes spirits share with the medicine man how they do such tricks, and a lot can be learned that way. In fact, most healing techniques used by shamans originally come from the spirits who shared how they do their work.

In family constellations, the representatives often take on the suffering of others in a direct way. For example, if someone was never able to express grief, the representative standing in his place may shed tears and suffer the pain of mourning in his place. Every inner shift a representative makes is a step taken for someone else; the representative is doing it for the other person. Because a representative does not usually personally know the individual he represents, there is little danger of taking on the suffering out of entanglements. Besides that, the representatives are chosen by somebody else to do the job, they cannot voluntarily choose to represent a specific person. A representative takes on suffering during the constellation, and afterwards, steps back into his own life, giving back the responsibility to the one he represented. Although the form of the constellation obviously differs from those of shamanic healing rituals, when suffering is taken on for others in order to help them, both constellations and old shamanic rituals make use of the same spiritual principles.

5. The Importance of Ancestral Strength

In systemic work, the strength that comes from ancestors has great importance. Ancestral strength gives purpose and direction to life, and it provides the power to accept and carry all kinds of difficulties. Many spiritual traditions teach that the strength the ancestors have to offer can be received by the living by simply giving the ancestors a place in their homes, and in their hearts. In many cultures, each house will have a small altar in it with some objects that represent the earlier generations. Incense, food, and drinks are placed on this altar every now and then; these are offerings for the ancestral spirits. In some Siberian tribes, the people of one household shared a box or small chest filled with ancestors in the form of tiny dolls. When a guest came in, his first question would be: "Are the old people at home?" The ancestors were taken out of the box and greeted; all dolls got a drop of vodka. Only then would the family and guests drink and eat. In most shamanic traditions, it is not just the earlier generations of the family that are considered as ancestors. However, in order to understand the shamanic images about ancestors, it is helpful to look at the element of fire first.

In the shamanic world view, fire is often the first and foremost life-giving power. Each fire, also the slow inner fire that keeps our bodies warm, is part of the fire of creation; the primordial force that brings being into existence. When you live, your physical body is warm because of your inner fire. When you die, you not only stop breathing, your temperature starts to drop and you become cold. The inner fire has gone out – or better: it has left with the soul when it withdrew from the physical body. In many shamanic (and Buddhist) cultures, a person that has stopped breathing is left untouched for some time, often hours, until the body is completely cold. Only then has the physical dying process been completed. Today medical science has confirmed that after breathing has stopped, there is no immediate death because electromagnetic brain patterns can still be measured for several hours. What these patterns mean is unknown, but we can be sure that the human brain stays active for several hours after the last breath has been exhaled.

The most important and basic teaching about fire is that it is composed of two different aspects. One aspect is flame; the other aspect is heat. Flame is the aspect that changes things, that transforms, that creates one thing out of another. The flame aspect of fire has a specific power that allows medicine people to perform certain types of healing. For example, with the help of flame, some traditional shamanic healers can mend broken bones in a matter of just days instead of many weeks. When you know how to apply flame, the physical substance of the body can be changed and transformed very fast. The other aspect of fire, heat, has a different nature. You can see heat as pure strength; strength that will flow into any vehicle that is made available for it. In shamanic healing practices, heat is not used to transform, but for example to boost the immune system and other self-regulating capacities of the body or psyche.

In traditional shamanism, the application of flame, transformation, is the responsibility of trained medicine people. It is considered dangerous for lay people to use it. The nature of flame is such that it will burn away all impurities when you are touched by it, and who can stand naked truth? That takes courage. If you meet truth unprepared, it can drive you insane. When you are touched by flame, impurities come to the surface and have to be dealt with in one way or another. The second aspect of fire however, heat, can be used by all because it can be felt, understood, and regulated more easily. Heat, which equals strength, is sought after and absorbed by everyone although it can also be dangerous when someone is exposed to it for too long. Too much heat, and the body and mind will suffer. Attuning to heat and absorbing the strength it carries becomes a direct and very intense experience when people join for prayers in purification ceremonies like the sweat lodge, which I described in chapter four. During this ceremony the heat can be very strong. The most obvious result is a very strong physical detoxification through perspiration, but the main purpose of the ceremony is to become strong through the intake of the life force that is released by the glowing red stones. Even babies and very old people come in, if only for a few minutes, and whenever somebody is sick or needs strength, a sweat lodge is organized for them. On the Native American reservations in the United States, sweat lodges are specially organized for alcohol and drug addicts. Many alcoholics and junkies sincerely wish to stop their addiction, but they lack strength to implement the decision to quit. In shamanic thinking, failure in life is more often diagnosed as a lack of strength than as a lack of (material or psychological) devices. Medicine people will try to get alcoholics and junkies together to pray in the sweat lodge where strength is added to the prayers through fire, through the power of the heated stones. Here, we meet an important shamanic paradigm: when strength is encountered, people need to pray; otherwise the strength that becomes available just flows into habitual patterns of thinking, and someone who is already in trouble might end up even more lost than he already was. You cannot encounter strength and act as if nothing special is happening – you may become ill or reinforce your weakness. It sounds like a paradox, but weakness can grow very strong too. Spiritual power in itself is blind, it is just energy and it can strengthen both health and disease. That is why it has to be directed carefully, and prayer has been found to be the best way to do this.

I could continue to explore the shamanic use and meaning of fire for a long time, but this is a chapter on ancestral strength. It suffices here to say that one of the foundations of traditional shamanism is the art of mastering fire in all its manifestations.

The basic division of fire into two separate qualities is so simple and obvious that most people overlook it, but it gains a significant dimension when you consider that according to the shamanic traditions, fire is the actual force of life, the substance of creation itself, and therefore is directly connected to our ancestors. Our ancestors are part of the creative life force since they have created us; they gave us life in the most literal sense. Since our ancestors are essentially our creators, they are part of the original life force, part of the fire of life. Since fire is separated into two aspects, the ancestors can also be separated into two groups. The flame aspect of the life force shapes us, and the heat aspect strengthens us. Our ancestors therefore both shape and strengthen us. The ones who shape us are our parents, grandparents, or others who raise us in childhood. They embody the flame aspect of the creative fire. They create our physical bodies, and direct the development of our personalities. They teach us language and consciously (and unconsciously) imprint us with emotional and ethical structures. The ancestors we have never met personally, but with whom we are unconsciously entangled, are also part of the flame. They too influence our emotions, our loyalties, our inner drives. The personality and physical body, which are created by flame, form a vehicle for strength. Strength (the heat aspect of the primordial fire) is brought in by the ancestors that did not directly shape us. These are the ancestors that are usually a minimum of three generations or more away from us. Pure strength is mostly supplied by those ancestors that did not have a direct influence on our lives. So, the actual form of the personality and the strength the personality is able to hold are two separate things. The two groups of ancestors are separate forces; they may work together in harmony or not. What shapes us does not necessarily supply us with strength, what strengthens us only shapes us limitedly.

Strength is what concerns people most in traditional shamanism; it is considered a medicine for almost any kind of discomfort, disease, or trouble. Where in systemic work unconscious entanglements are seen as one of the root causes of many problems, and people try to free themselves from these entanglements in order to find health, the shamanic approach is to look for power when you feel bad. People in trouble will try to find new supplies of strength so that they can grow strong once more, and when they are strong they feel good again. This focus on strength is one of the reasons why in traditional shamanism, there are but few rituals and structures for healing problems that are the result of systemic entanglements. Entanglements are often simply bypassed by focussing on finding strength. This strategy can be noted in all shamanic cultures. It can be understood when the original nomadic lifestyle of shamanic people is taken into account. All the members of a nomadic family were completely dependent on each other; only by working together as a smooth functioning whole could the individual members survive. In such a small and closed system, a direct confrontation is simply too serious a threat for survival of the greater unit and therefore should be avoided at all costs, especially in winter times when everybody stays in the tent for days, weeks, or even months at a time. In the nomadic shamanic cultures, there are all kinds of social codes that aim at avoiding the confrontations that to us would seem unavoidable in a situation where people live very closely together. Tradition dictates which family members never address each other directly. Just one example, a woman who had married into a certain family would move into the tent of her husband, but in many cultures she would never look her father-in-law straight in the eye or speak to him. When trouble and tensions arose, traditional people would not confront each other. Instead, they would try to find the strength to deal with it and carry it so that they would be able to continue to function as a whole and the family would not fall apart.

The ancestors are an important source of strength in traditional shamanic life. One way to make sure that entanglements are bypassed and everybody has enough resources of ancestral strength is that children are taught to see all people as their relatives. One of my own traditional teachers, himself an old man now, told me how his great-grandfather instructed him to never think of people as other than relatives. "Even when you call someone you don't know, never say 'Hey, you', always say 'Hey, brother', or 'Hey, sister'." Visiting a Native American friend, I am not introduced to people I do not know as a stranger, but as 'my Dutch relative'. Your sense of belonging increases profoundly when you call all people with gray hair grandfather or grandmother, all people in middle age aunt and uncle, everybody your own age brother and sister, the ones younger than you little brother, little sister, nephew or niece. More strength and support can be found than just through your own family of origin. And although this extra strength may not be as powerful or influential as the strength that can be received through the direct ancestors, at least all of it is available since there are relatively few entanglements possible with the members of an extended family. Another quite elegant shamanic strategy to bypass the effect of entanglements and subsequent blocks in the flow of ancestral strength is that not only humans are considered as ancestors. In many shamanic cultures, people are taught that the family descends from an animal. So, some families are raven people, bear people, or otter people, and there are many more possibilities. Even in Scotland there were clans that said they originated from animals, for example from the wild cat. These are powerful images, since animal species consist mostly of healthy adults and young, not of the sick and dying. When an animal is sick, it is usually killed and eaten within hours by other species; this leaves us humans with the impression that animals are forever strong and healthy. For someone who sees the bear as his original ancestor, a bear claw on a string around his neck is a very powerful thing; it is part of the body of his own blood, his own ancestor. A dream of a bear is a gift from the elders; it is not talked about and kept in the soul, having the power to sustain the dreamer for years or even a lifetime. Seeing animals as ancestors can be seen as a symbolic way of going back in time to a period of history when the ancestors were not even truly human. Such ancestors have no individuality and are just part of nature, just like wild animals are today. As such, they are perfect vehicles for the heat aspect of the fire that is the creative force, the heat that carries strength.

Although the two aspects of the creative fire have a different nature, and can be seen and known independently of each other, fire is still one element. Flame and heat, form and strength, intermingle. From a certain perspective, they cannot really be distinguished from each other. When there is enough heat, flame arises spontaneously, and flames will in their turn create heat. The two are always interwoven, and the life force is not complete when you have only one of them. The two types of ancestors can overlap, and they have to balance each other; both groups are needed. If all goes well, and parents gradually stop directing the lives of their maturing children, they can, from the perspective of the child, gradually grow closer to the group of older ancestors. If parents are able to support their children to truly stand on their own two feet, they will gradually start to embody heat instead of flame. Then they do not give shape anymore; they become a strong link between their children and the distant ancestors.

Once I was on one of the Native American reservations in the USA, and I was invited to participate in an all night healing ceremony performed for a young girl. The grandmother and great-grandmother of the girl had initiated the ceremony, but her mother did not believe in the traditional healing ceremonies and did not want to participate. Still, in the early morning when the actual healing part of the ceremony was over, the mother came in silently and sat next to her daughter for half an hour. It was obvious that her presence helped the girl to really take in and integrate the good things that had come to her via her grandmother and great-grandmother. The image of the generations standing in line, supporting each other, has a great strengthening force, and it is also used in systemic work. During a constellation, it might happen that someone has no power to take his own place, and therefore cannot face up to the challenges of his life and fate. In other constellations, healing movements simply stop because of the weakness of a key representative. One of the possible solutions a facilitator may offer in such situations is bringing in an ancestral lineage by adding representatives to the constellation. When a man needs strength, male representatives are chosen; when it concerns a woman, female representatives are needed. Three or four people of the same gender will stand in a row behind the one who is weak, representing the father, grandfather, and great-grandfather or the mother, grandmother, and great-grandmother. The representative who needed strength is encouraged to feel and absorb the strength that is coming to him through this line, and he soon feels more powerful. The constellation can then proceed; the healing movement that had to be interrupted can be completed. When, in constellations, the older generations are asked to simply just support and bless the younger ones, an immediate healing force starts to flow which helps all the representatives.

6. The Experience of Timelessness

During a shamanic healing ceremony, the habitual perception of time is broken very skillfully. A quality of timelessness is experienced by all who participate: client, shaman, and spectators. The shift from linear time to a sense of timelessness can be compared to entering a hot bath. Entering the hot water with a familiar sense of relaxation, your tensions dissolve and you enjoy the experience as your body recognizes the sensation of the hot water on your skin. Regardless of whether you take baths every day or just once a month, regardless of whether you use the same bathtub today as yesterday, when the water has the right temperature and you close your eyes and step in, the moment you slip into the water it feels just like any other bath you ever took, it's like you're back there. The timelessness of shamanic ritual is 'entered' in a similar way; you slip into a familiar experience that seems to have been waiting for you. In shamanic context, various factors contribute to this shift of awareness. Singing is one of the most important ones. There are different types of shamanic healing and purification rituals, and sequences of specific songs belong to each of them. During the longer ceremonies, such series of songs are repeated again and again, always accompanied by the same monotonous drumming. Many of the more intense healing rituals are (at least partially) done in darkness. Immersed in darkness, hearing and singing the old familiar prayer songs and feeling the loud drums resonating on your skin, the experience of time somehow becomes mixed with the experience of space. In darkness you cannot see the borders of space anymore; space is still felt but it has become undefined. In much the same way, you are surrounded by timelessness: time still exists but you have your lost grip on it. The perception of outer darkness changes into awareness of an inner place. The experience of timelessness is deepened and strengthened with each successive ritual, because in each ritual, the same type of continuous and powerful sensory imprinting is used. The inner experience of timelessness can be revisited again and again.

Loosing track of linear time is one of the characteristics of trance, both of light and deep trances. People enter trances very easily, and basically any longer rhythmic sensory input induces it. Someone may enter a trance sitting in a train with closed eyes, listening to the sound of the wheels in the tracks, while dancing at a party to a continuous beat and pulsating lights, even during a good massage. As soon as someone relaxes and is exposed to rhythmic sensory input for some minutes, he will gradually enter a light trance. In a trance, the ability to measure time, which is quite accurate in daily life, is fairly easily disrupted. After having been in a trance, regardless of whether the trance was light or deep, most people express surprise at how little or how much time has passed. The experience of timelessness that is cultivated in shamanic practice is not simply lacking the ability to measure time correctly; it can be compared with the sensation of vigor and health. For some people, 'health' simply means an absence of disease or discomfort. Health is then defined as a negative condition. Others actually experience health as an energy, a presence of vitality and strength. In the same way, someone can only experience a disabled ability to measure linear time, a condition that is a natural effect of trance. Attention can also be trained to focus deeper and deeper, and then timelessness becomes not just an absence of linear time, but a distinct presence of something else; something which feels good, full, and rich.

The experience of timelessness is of paramount importance in shamanic practice. When the linear experience of time is broken, the flow of the stories we constantly tell ourselves in our minds is disrupted. Stories about the past, about what is going on now or should be going on instead; about what happened yesterday or what should happen in the future; thinking along these lines is only possible as long as awareness is firmly anchored in linear time. In the timelessness of shamanic ritual, these inner stories soon loose their anchor. They become fragmented and lose cohesion; there may even be moments when they are totally silenced. As soon as the compulsive inner monologue is weakened, consciousness starts to free up for a new experience. When the inner stories about ourselves and others have lost their grip on our attention, what we start to feel is the actual experience of the energy linked to these stories, the energy that is their essence. For example, instead of repeating the endless familiar complaint about how your partner never says he loves you, you may simply suddenly feel another truth; the silent suffering which closed his heart long ago. Or, instead of telling yourself again and again how your mother never really saw you and how that irritates you, you now sense the mindless fear of a very young child that sometimes needed more than his parents could give. Habitual patterns of thinking serve to keep 'reality' fixed in a form that serves the identifications of the personality. Anchored in timelessness, consciousness starts to see another layer of truth; that of the actual energy in the body and the deeper layers of the psyche.

Experiencing timelessness, and in this way opening up for more essential layers of experience is a key factor in healing, both for the shaman and his client. A shaman or medicine man is not always doing healing work; that would be unhealthy for him. If shamans were not able to anchor themselves firmly in ordinary physical reality after their meetings with the spirits, they would soon become ill or psychotic. In daily life, the attention is directed to the world of matter, but when the shaman leads a ceremony, he should be able to direct his attention totally to the world of spirit, otherwise he will not be able to do his work. The shaman disconnects from daily life by allowing his consciousness to sink deeper and deeper into timelessness, and when the ceremony is over, he returns to a linear perception of time. For the client, it is also important to be able to enter a state of timelessness. At some point during a shamanic healing ritual, when the drumming and singing have been going on for some time, the shaman or medicine man will ask the client to pray out loud and ask the spirits for help. Shamanic prayers are always improvised, and the client, already in a light trance, starts praying. He may start out with his usual thoughts, but as the prayer continues, these thoughts drift away, and deeper, more essential feelings come to the surface. Speaking out with a clear voice about these more fundamental truths and experiences is essential. The client's identification with his disease can only start to change when he literally gives voice to the underlying structures of thinking and feeling. At some point during the prayers, a client reaches a moment when he is far away from his habitual way of describing his problem. He continues to ask the spirits for help and his mind and senses are open wide. Then, he finishes his prayers because he starts to feel empty; in fact he is now in a purified state, depleted of stories, in contact with his soul. Only at that point can the actual healing work start.

In timelessness, the spirits become visible easily. When the mind has stopped its habitual ways of entertaining itself, the senses start to open up more, first for the physical environment but then for the spiritual layers. To make sure the shaman can see the spirit world, many shamanic ceremonies are performed partly in darkness after the trance has been induced. In darkness, the eyes of the shaman are not distracted anymore by the physical world. If light is needed during the ceremony, for example because the shaman's assistants need it to perform their tasks, the shaman may choose to wear a blindfold himself so his eyes are shielded from the light. In the meantime, continuous drumming and singing create an auditory sensory overload, and this deepens the shaman's trance. In the darkness, images start to appear by themselves. After some time of exposure to continuous loud monotonous drumming, the mind cannot process the auditory input anymore. Everything may suddenly seem strangely silent, or the shaman may hear voices and sounds that are not part of the songs. Sometimes beautiful songs are heard, and many of the shaman's songs are found in this way, when the shaman is deep in trance and listens to the drums. Such spontaneous visual and auditory hallucinations are a sign that a certain shift of consciousness is happening. Through training, shamans can learn to deepen and control this state to an amazing extent, and in it, they can have consistent and clear communication with their spirit helpers. Siberian shamans also use their shaman costume to enter a trance. When the shaman dances in his costume, the iron bells and hangers on it make quite a loud noise, and thus help to create an auditory sensory overload. A shaman costume may weigh twenty or thirty kilograms, and dancing with such a heavy weight is extremely tiring. After just minutes of dancing, a shaman may already be exhausted, and in this state, habitual patterns of thinking dissolve very easily.

As one learns to direct awareness more and more precisely, the experience of timelessness feels more and more like being connected to a presence or an aspect of an inner consciousness which exists all the time; as if a part of us is always in timelessness and our attention can be linked to that aspect of ourselves. In the process of entering timelessness, familiar ways of thinking make way for awareness of the deeper layers of truth beneath these habitual patterns of thinking. Deeper and deeper layers can be unraveled, and finally there is just silence. Our soul exists in the silence of timelessness, and in timelessness, we can, to a certain extent, become aware of it. As long as we are rooted in the timeless part of ourselves, our personality will have difficulty maintaining its grip on thoughts and emotions. However, in a timeless state, the personality is also unable to enter the inner room of our being where our soul can be found. The personality can stay at the door, looking in, and to a certain extent, it can get a glimpse or a taste of what is going on there, but it will never be able to fully step in.

Timelessness is not just a state of consciousness; it is also the experience of an inner place where our inner soul can be found and experienced. Whatever we experience during trance, in timelessness, can somehow be kept or stored in that space, in our soul. One of the important principles understood and used in shamanic healing is that a healing image created during a ritual should not be stored in the personality but in the soul. In this way, it stays safely out of reach of habitual ways of thinking.

It is easy to understand this idea of a memory being stored either in the personality, where it is subject to normal thinking, or being kept in a place of timelessness that is part of the soul, where it will remain intact. Imagine you come home from a fantastic vacation. You have taken photos during most of the highlights. However, as you talk repeatedly about your vacation to various friends and members of your family, and you show your photos again and again to others, you notice that your actual memories are gradually replaced by the stories that you tell. The more you talk about your vacation, the harder it gets to really feel how it actually was. The more you look at your photos, the less other visual images remain. In the end, the stories and photos are all that you have left; the memories of what you actually experienced are gone. Imagine that during this particular holiday you once made love with a wonderful man you met on the beach. You spent a day and a night with him. The two of you had dinner with candlelight on the beach, and had sex in the moonlight on the warm sand. The memories of this are very special and you do not talk about them to others, except maybe one or two of your best friends, and only rarely. There are moments when you think back, and you can feel again the warm breeze on your skin as you were lying naked on the sand; you can really still feel the touch of his hand on your arms, your back. The memory of this treasured adventure does not diminish in time – long after all the other memories of your vacation have been replaced by stories connected to photos – this particular experience has kept its freshness. That was possible because you have not told many people about the actual experience, you have protected it well. You have managed to store it in a special inner place and have kept it there. It has stayed alive because you have not replaced it with stories about it. You took it out of the linear mind and personality and kept it in timelessness. Stored there, it can continue to be a source of strength for years to come.

When the true memory of a healing experience is replaced by stories the personality makes of the experience, it is not just that you gradually forget what actually happened: as you replace the actual experience with new images, you also lose access to a source of energy. However, when you manage to keep the image of a powerful and healing experience in timelessness, your soul embraces it. The image then becomes a vehicle for a healing power that comes from your own soul. When the personality is the guardian of a memory, the memory loses power quickly, but when it is kept in the soul, the experience actually gains strength because the soul adds power to it.

For the shamanic practitioner, learning to be silent about important personal experiences with the spirits is an essential aspect of the training. There are gifts of the spirits that must be stored in the soul as healing images. This can be applied to the memory of a family constellation too. When the memory of a family constellation that has come to a resolution is gradually replaced by the stories the mind creates about the experience, the memory of the constellation is subject to change. This changing image is progressively less and less connected to the actual experience, and as the two drift apart, less and less power can flow through it. The mind carefully remolds the experience into something that only serves to support a continuation of its fixed patterns of thinking. However, when the memory of a constellation is stored in timelessness, it is protected from the analysis of the mind that is grounded in linear time, and it does not change. The original healing impulse then continues to stimulate a process of change long after the actual constellation was set up. At a certain moment however, after a few months or after a longer period of time, a memory that was kept in the soul may disappear, or rather, no more power of the soul flows through it. This is usually a good sign. The soul simply lets a healing image go when the work that could be done through it is completed. At that point, someone is free to start talking about the experience to family and friends; the experience does not need the protection of the soul anymore.

    I would like to give a concrete example of how a healing image can be kept in timelessness until it finally results in a healing which touches both levels of the soul and the personality. In March 1999, I was participating in a seminar with Bert Hellinger and Hunter Beaumont in San Francisco. I had discussed with Bert Hellinger some experiences I had had with physical violence of aggressors I had been exposed to, and had also mentioned certain moments in my life when I had been at the very threshold of death after serious illnesses. Then, during a tea break, he suggested two exercises for me. One was to visualize going into the world of the dead and looking for the murderers. There, I should visualize that I lie down with them, then look at them and say: "I am one of you." The second was an exercise to see death not in front of me but behind me, and to take every day as an extra, a blessing. However, after describing these exercises to me, he enigmatically said: "Don't do these exercises, don't sit down to do them. Your soul will know how to take care of them." It did not sound like a therapeutical intervention to me. Being trained in shamanism, I automatically took this suggestion as a traditional shamanic instruction, and followed it accordingly. I literally put the suggestions in my soul, that part of myself that continuously exists in the silence of timelessness. I did not just store the images the exercises provoked in me, but also the actual image of Bert Hellinger explaining them to me, the position in which he stood, my own physical sensations as I listened to his description of the exercises, even the smell in the room. I kept the whole experience unchanged and never thought about it in an analytical sense or told anyone about it. I kept it alive by sometimes, during a ritual, re-experiencing this moment. Then, a few months after the seminar, I had a very powerful dream.

In the dream, I was part of some kind of group or entity that had killed a number of people. Since I had been a member of the group, I had been participating in the killing. I was standing in court when the dream started, and it was time for my defense. I had decided to be my own defender instead of taking a lawyer, although I knew that nobody had ever done this before. When it was my turn to speak, I gave a short and simple speech. I said I was guilty of the crimes, and that I accepted the consequences of this. I told the court that the only defense I had is that I was a human being. I told them that every human is capable of terrible deeds, and that only the circumstances of our lives determine whether we will be allowed to become decent people or will become monsters. I had become a killer, but there was no true difference between me and all the people present in court; I was still the same as everybody else. As I said this I was calm, I felt ready to accept judgment and in this way take responsibility for my actions. The judge decided: the death penalty would be executed in a few weeks. The dream then stretched on; I experienced days and nights. I wrote letters to those I loved, spoke to family and friends, prepared myself for death. I was calm; sometimes I cried and grieved, but I became more and more clear. Finally, the last morning arrived. I woke up, and everything I did had this strange acute quality; everything was crystal clear. I washed my hands, brushed my teeth, knowing I would be dead in just a few hours. After some time, I was taken to the electric chair. As I sat in the waiting room, I felt death so close to me, so mysterious; everything became so vivid and direct, so intense and calm at the same time. As I sat there waiting, I was told that the execution was postponed. Then another type of waiting began, taking hours; the acuteness and calmness stayed, anchoring deeper and deeper. Finally I was told that the judge had reconsidered my case and I would be released. I would live; instead of being killed I would be banned. I was released immediately, the doors of the prison opened and I was standing in a wide and open landscape, sunny and dry. I only had my clothes and some money to buy a ticket to get out of the country. I had left everything and everybody behind and had in some strange way survived dying. I had become another person. I felt no more innocence and no more guilt; there was just awareness and strength. I woke up from this dream and continued to function in this state of calmness, acuteness. Colors were more vivid; everything had a sort of slow motion quality since I had a very clear awareness of everything. My heartbeat was slow and strong. For some days my attention had this focussed quality and I was constantly aware of being alive, having been given more time to live. Of course after some days I started to feel more like my usual self again, but something had been truly transformed.

Essentially, a healing process had started the moment I understood Bert Hellinger's instruction to let my soul take care of the exercises by storing an experience in the inner space of timelessness. Of course, I had no way of knowing what the final effect would be when the healing power of my own soul started to work through the image of being given these instructions. I simply allowed the memory of the experience in San Francisco to continue to work on me, unchanging, never changing it or allowing it to lose energy by talking about it. Something was bound to happen sooner or later. The dream I finally had was essentially the final manifestation of a healing movement, the grounding of a healing process that had been happening invisibly. Only after the dream did I start to think about it all, and I had some valuable insights that were intellectually helpful. I understood for example, that my exposure to violence had made me feel totally defenseless and lost, and that in my attempts to find my own strength again, I had started to feel superior to aggressors in general. I had started to think I was a better person than people who were violent, and that made me feel powerful again. In this way, I was creating a strong shadow though, since I could only maintain this self-image as long as I was denying the existence of my own violent impulses. I had to return to the aggressors, and acknowledge that essentially I was no different from them. These kinds of insights could only come up after having the dream. The spiritual healing being completed, the memory of being given these instructions did not need to be kept in timelessness anymore: I could now start to use my analytical mind to find additional truths and inspiration.

In a seminar on family constellations, a natural use of the factor of timelessness can be observed. The presence of the dead, the unborn, and even abstract concepts breaks down the usual experience of time. Participants are soon captivated by the constellations and are drawn into the intense experiences of the representatives. In an empathic concentration, borders dissolve and people lose track of time. There are long periods of silence interrupted by short archaic sentences with a high emotional and spiritual charge. In this environment, the shift to the experience of timelessness happens gradually, and it is a spontaneous phenomenon that is hardly noticed since it is so natural. However in effect, almost everybody who participates in a seminar of family constellations spends most of the time in a light trance.

When a healing movement has been found and completed, a constellation finishes. Ideally, the client then looks at the overall image of the constellation. Seeing the representatives, now balanced in their new positions, ideally he puts this image in a deep place inside himself. The image has to be kept in a protected space so it can continue to do its healing work, supported by the soul. If the constellation is looked at only from the perspective of habitual judgment, the memory of it cannot have more than a superficial quality. So, just like after a shamanic healing, someone who has set up a constellation must be able to somehow stay focused in timelessness in order to store the healing image in the right place. Many clients who have set up a constellation of their families however have not actively developed such skills, and this leaves it up to the intuitive understanding of the client whether he will be able to 'take the healing' or not – unless the facilitator intervenes.

A facilitator of family constellations does not consciously employ methods to guide the participants in the seminar into a trance. However, references are sometimes made to the experience of timelessness and the importance of keeping experiences in this inner place. After a constellation, a facilitator may say something like "I trust your good soul to take care of it", as Bert Hellinger sometimes does, which can be seen as a reference to the quality of timelessness where the experience can be left intact. Also, an instruction like "Don't speak about the constellation afterwards" is actually a suggestion to refrain from creating stories about the experience. When there is no story, the image will not change and remains intact; when a healing image remains intact, the soul can add strength to it. The suggestions I mentioned are in essence related to helping people to stay out of their habitual linear experience of time. Family constellations are only possible in a timeless field, but this is not usually explained to the participants in a seminar and so they are not clearly guided to enhance and maintain the specific state of awareness of timelessness. Many facilitators have observed that after a constellation, some clients are able to absorb the healing image, and that there are others who are obviously not able to do this. My observation is that knowing, or not knowing the inner spaces that exist in timelessness determines whether people are able to take in the healing power of a constellation or not. People who cannot take the healing image in are usually unable to do this because they continue to habitually think (or speak) about what they have seen, using for example, the language of psychotherapy to analyze and explain the constellation. They are doing their best in their own way to take in what the constellation has shown them, but they are unable to leave the healing image intact in the process; they need to take it apart through analysis. In this way, they lose access to the power that the constellation makes accessible when it is stored in the soul.

There are certain things a facilitator can do when he notices a client is firmly anchored in an analytical frame of mind, which is a sign of being in a linear time frame. It would probably not be helpful to switch off the lights and bring in shamanic drums to sing ritual songs; such specific shamanic ways of handling trances take some time to master, usually at least a few years. Many Westerners however have experience with various forms of meditation and relaxation exercises, and some of these might be helpful. A facilitator can, for example, at the end of a constellation, guide the client in a short meditation. He can ask the client to notice the facial expressions of the representatives to bring awareness first in the here and now, and then suggest to the client to feel the sensations in his own body as he remembers what processes have unfolded. Asking the client to ground himself in his body, he could suggest breathing the image of the constellation in, bringing the image to a silent place in his heart. He can suggest paying attention to the atmosphere and power of the constellation, and ask the client to visualize this in the form of a field of very subtle matter that can be inhaled and absorbed. Then, when the client has done this, and sits for a minute with his eyes closed, allowing the exercise to affect his energy, the facilitator could ask him to refrain from speaking about the constellation for a few weeks to protect it for some time like a fragile treasure. Such simple suggestions, which do not have to take up more than a few minutes time, are often beneficial for those clients that have difficulty taking a constellation in.

The facilitator should however continue to be respectful at all times. Sometimes it is absolutely right for a client to not yet embrace the constellation because he may simply need more time to accept it.

7. Manifestations of the Soul and the Spirit

In previous chapters, the words spirit and soul have been used several times. 'Spirit' has been used to describe a shaman's helper: a conscious entity with individual awareness that does not live in a physical body. For the shaman, a spirit is a concrete presence; it is possible to communicate with it in a trance. Up until now, I have used the word soul to describe an inner presence that can be found through the deepening experience of timelessness. The words soul and spirit basically indicate the same type of awareness, being of human nature or not. According to the shamanic traditions, not only humans, but also animals, plants, rocks and water have a soul or spirit too. A spirit is a soul, and a soul is a spirit. When this consciousness resides in a physical body, it is usually called a soul. When it has no physical body, it is usually called a spirit, and so the souls of people who have died are often called spirits too.

A true and complete understanding of the soul is probably beyond the grasp of our intellect, just as it is not possible to really understand the nature of the power that created our universe. The descriptions and images we use to indicate the nature of the soul are necessarily limited, but still they can help us to learn and understand more about our own spiritual nature. What I am looking for in the following exploration is not a complete understanding of the mysteries that the soul presents us with, but I simply want to create an image of the soul and the spirit that is helpful in the context of the family constellations. To start to construct such an image, I believe it is useful to first describe some personal experiences of my perception of the souls of people who have died.

Some time ago, I did a private session for a man who was addicted to gambling, I will call him John. John told me that both his father and brother had been professional gamblers, and both had died quite young. His father had died in poverty; his brother had been killed by a criminal organization from which he had borrowed a large sum of money that he could not pay back. John did not have a gambling problem while his brother was still alive, but lost control soon after his brother was killed. Gambling, for a long time just an occasional pastime, became compulsive. He felt that he was taking over the self-destructive patterns of his father and brother, as if some kind of dark energy was moving through the family and now he was the next in line to become the victim of it. The way he described it showed that he knew something about family entanglements. However, I told him that my impression of his situation differed from his, and that in my view, his obsessive gambling was actually an expression of unconscious loyalty. Both John's father and brother had died lonely, without support, and somehow John was drawn to them as if he would still be able to do something to support them. Being a gambler himself now, he had become in some strange way very close to his father and brother. Obviously, gambling was the only way he knew how to be near to them. I suggested a small ritual for John – to put photos of the two dead men in front of him, and a set of playing cards or another symbol for gambling in between the photos and himself. I asked him to close his eyes and visualize doing the ritual while I described it, so that he would not forget how to do it. I suggested he should speak to his father's and brother's photos as if the men were really there, telling them he wanted them to still be part of his life, but that until now, the only way he knew how to be close to them was by copying their gambling. Now he could see that this was not going to be helpful, neither for his father and brother nor for himself. I told John to ask their blessing or permission for him to give up gambling, so he would be free to remember them in another, more healthy way. Next I suggested that John address the symbol for gambling, as if it were a person. He could tell it that he had thought about getting closer to his loved ones through gambling, but that he saw this only created more destruction and so it was time to move on. Now he was ready to try another way of loving and honoring them. Then, I suggested he should simply move the symbol away and get rid of it by burning it or throwing it in a river. As John was visualizing all of this, his brother's spirit appeared next to us. I could not see him clearly, but I felt him all the stronger. As John opened up for the healing movement of the ritual, I could feel his brother silently giving his blessing and support. It was a simple and pure gesture, John's heart was touched deeply and responded to his brother's presence, although he could not see him, and I had not told him that his brother had actually come in. We closed the session. A few hours later, John called me. After the session he had gone home, and he had suggested to his wife that they go and take a walk on the beach, where he could then tell her about the session. When they had walked up to their car, which was parked in the street, a man had been standing next to it. As they got nearer, the man had turned his face to them, and both had recognized John's brother. He had looked at them, then turned and stepped around the corner that was just meters away. John's wife immediately ran after him, but found the street around the corner completely empty; only seconds after they had clearly seen him, John's brother had disappeared, he was simply gone. John and his wife were astonished. John's wife, when they had seen the apparition of the brother, had not yet been informed about what had happened at the session.

Recently, when I was a participant in a family constellation seminar, I had another experience in which a spirit was present. A woman had set up a constellation, and the facilitator was not able to find a resolution, something was missing. It was not clear how a resolution could be found, and so I tried to see if I could get a sense of what was going on by checking the room for the presence of spirits who were connected to the family. One of the grandfathers who was represented in the constellation was considered a hero, he had been a volunteer as a life guard on the seashore and he had helped rescue a number of swimmers in trouble and sailors from sinking ships. To my surprise, I saw a spirit standing next to this grandfather. This spirit, a dead man, was obviously not represented in the constellation. In silence, my eyes closed, and unnoticed by the other participants and the facilitator, I concentrated on the spirit and asked him what he was doing there. I understood that he had been left behind on a sinking ship because the grandfather had not dared to take more than a certain number of men in his boat during a rescue operation – although the grandfather's boat was actually big enough to rescue more men considering the fact that the weather had not been extremely bad. Together with two others, the man I saw had been left on the sinking ship and they had drowned. It had been planned that they would be picked up by another rescue team, but the boat had sunk before that help could reach them. One of my own spirit helpers interrupted the communication at this point and told me I should not continue to speak directly to this spirit. I should not get involved since I was not leading the seminar. I said goodbye to the dead man, and focused my attention on my helper instead. He explained that the grandfather had done much good work, but in fact he was not very far from being a murderer too. He had not actually killed the three men, but had consciously left them in an extremely dangerous situation while there were other options. Because of this, he carried responsibility for their deaths. The grandfather had never spoken about this event, and the guilt he had felt was therefore never recognized in the family. The responsibility for the death of the three men went unclaimed, and thus caused trouble for the next generations in this family. I did not speak about my observations to the facilitator; it was the first time I was participating in his seminar and I could not know if this type of information would be welcomed by him.

In these two cases, I have described three different types of manifestations of spirits. In the first case, the soul of the dead brother was initially only a distinct presence that could be felt, but some hours later he was temporarily clothed in a body that seemed to be physical to the people that saw it. In the second case, a dead man was presenting himself in yet another way; none of the other participants in the seminar felt a presence or saw anything, still, with my 'inner' eyes I had clearly seen a man and could communicate with him easily. These three different ways of manifestations – a felt presence, a subtle body that can only be perceived in trance, and a denser body that is visible to others in daily consciousness – are typical examples of experiences with spirits. It is not only possible to have such encounters with spirits, but also with the souls of people who are still alive. The human soul can occasionally manifest aspects of itself in a variety of ways outside of the physical body. It is not so strange that it can do this; the soul is after all of the same nature as the spirits. In subsequent chapters I will explore this phenomenon further.

A soul or a spirit must obviously be clothed in some kind of body, no matter how subtle, otherwise it cannot be noticed by others. Occasionally, as in the first case I described, the spirit's body seems to closely resemble physical matter and it can be seen by people in normal waking consciousness. However, such a manifestation is relatively rare; it is much more common that a spirit can only be noticed after an effort has been made. Someone in a trance, attuned to his own soul, can notice the spirits relatively easy, clothed in a body of a subtle nature. Regardless of whether the spirit's body seems to have a dense or very subtle quality, it always seems to be made of some kind of matter, of a substance. Based on my personal experiences, I would say that a spirit (or a soul of a living person that has temporarily manifested itself outside of the physical body) can express itself through various substances. Or, more accurately: it seems to me that spirits and free wandering souls can be experienced by our senses when they are clothed in various substances.

My own experiences until now have lead me to believe that individual souls or spirits are made of a certain energy which can only be directly experienced by us as an aspect of our own consciousness, for example, during certain meditative states, or when we are grounded in the timelessness of trance. Although we can experience our own soul inside ourselves as pure consciousness, our physical or subtle senses cannot perceive the actual souls or spirits around us. When we look inwards we find the soul, but when we look outwards it evades us. Many people have seen manifestations of spirits and souls, but who has seen 'pure soul'? What we see when we perceive the spirits are their temporary bodies, the 'clothes' they wear. Some people can see various kinds of subtle energy, which could theoretically be manifestations of the soul, possibly even be the soul in its pure state. However, we cannot communicate directly with 'energy'. Energy can be read or interpreted, but it is not possible to talk with it. I do not think that the energy, the souls and spirits we can sometimes see manifested around us are truly the essence of the soul. However, no matter how impossible it might be to understand the actual substance of the soul itself, it is relatively easy to relate to the bodies in which souls and spirits appear to our senses.

Souls and spirits can only be perceived when they are clothed in temporary subtle bodies. A living man's soul lives in a physical body. But where do the spirits reside? There must be some kind of place or zone somewhere where they are at home; they have to live somewhere. Where could that be? In shamanism, the question is relevant because the advice of spirits is often sought. If you want to reach the spirits you need to know where to reach them. If, so to speak, you do not know their address, you cannot ring their doorbell or write them a letter. The shamanic traditions say the spirits live in their own world, and this world of spirit is linked to our physical world. The typical shamanic symbol is that of a layered universe, in which the various worlds are connected by the world tree that grows through all of them. The shaman can perceive this tree while he is in a trance, and can somehow climb up and down this tree to visit the various spirit worlds. The image I personally use when I think about the different worlds and their relation to the nature of the soul is that of radio waves. Human consciousness can be compared with a radio that is able to pick up frequencies from various stations. I imagine it simple; for example, that on frequency 100, there is a certain spirit world, on frequency 105, we have the physical world, on 110, another spirit world, and so on. The world of the spirits is not a place, but a frequency. In this model, the different worlds can occupy the same space at the same time, in the form of various frequencies. The different frequencies of the radio waves could be compared with the subtle matter the spirits use to show themselves to us. When we listen to the radio, we can hear voices of people that are far away from us. In the same way, when we are in trance we can tune our consciousness to various frequencies and see the manifestations of spirits that exist on the different levels. But just as we, in the physical world, see physical bodies without seeing the actual souls that live in them, so we can see the spirits in their various worlds without seeing the actual substance of their soul. What we see in the other worlds are temporary bodies, while the spirit's essential nature continues to be out of our senses' grasp.

The idea that spirits must make use of a *temporary body* in order to make themselves understood is one of the most important paradigms of shamanic practice. All shamanic traditions help the spirits to manifest themselves during ceremonies by offering them a temporary body. When offered a temporary body, the spirits do not have to create one themselves. Physical objects are used for this, spiritually cleansed by prayers, herbs, and/or other purifying agents. The colored flags that are part of many shamanic altars all over the subarctic regions are sometimes called robes: a robe for the spirit to wear. On Siberian shamans' ritual costumes there are many temporary bodies for the spirits, images of people and animals made in iron by a blacksmith. The flags on the altar, the images on the shaman costume – through them, the spirits can enter the ceremony and make themselves felt.

Shamanic practitioners may also actively help spirits to manifest themselves during rituals by supplying them with extra energy. Shamans make sure they have a lot of energy before they go into a ceremony; the spirits may use some of the shaman's energy to manifest themselves more clearly. The shaman's energy may for example, be increased by fasting and refraining from sexual activity for some days before a ritual starts. When advanced shamanic practitioners have prepared themselves well, and meet up for a few days of intense rituals, the spirits sometimes manifest themselves in remarkable ways. The spirits are invited through continuous prayers, and their subtle bodies are strengthened in this way: prayer directs energy. The spirits may come in during the ritual and show themselves in the form of random lights, or as groups of sparks floating around in the room. When they show up in this form, they do not usually speak. Sometimes the spirits are invisible but they can still touch people; this feels like a real physical touch – warm and strong. For the inexperienced shamanic practitioner this is initially an unsettling experience! Animal spirits come in sometimes, looking like physical animals; sometimes they talk like humans. Spirits will sometimes lift objects off the ground and move them through the air, for all to see. Often they show themselves only to individuals, but there may also be moments when they are visible for many people at the same time. Although the spirits are able to manifest themselves in remarkable ways, it is not the cast that every shamanic ritual is a spiritual circus. In fact, it is more likely than not that during a few days of ceremony, there are just one or two manifestations of spirit, of a more or less subtle nature. Usually, the spirits will manifest themselves just to the medicine people or shamans, to bring some answers to the prayers that have been said.

By understanding the spirits' use of temporary bodies, traditional shamans learned how to improve the communication with the spirits. However before communication can start, the spirits first have to arrive, they need to be called in. How can a shaman reach the spirits when he needs their help? How to send a message from one world to the other? Some old Lakota songs describe it beautifully. During ceremonies, songs are addressed to the spirits. Calling songs invite the spirits; healing songs ask them for help, departing songs say goodbye. In a certain departing song that is used in the sweat lodge ceremony, participants in the ritual sing together the words that the spirits have often said when they left a ceremony. "We are leaving now, we retreat again until we are voice distance away." The human voice is the bridge to the spirits; it can reach the spirits in their own world. When there is a need for the presence of the spirits, or when a message needs to be given to them, people can use their voice and speak out loud. Shamans use their voices to speak to let the spirits know they are needed. I have never met a traditional shamanic practitioner, no matter which tradition, who did not invite the spirits by spoken words, in prayers and songs.

The spiritual principles that have shaped shamanic practice are also at work during the process of setting up a family constellation. In a constellation, the representatives offer their physical bodies as temporary bodies to other souls and spirits. That sounds rather archaic, and in fact it is. When you look at the process of setting up a family constellation with traditional shamanism in mind, a constellation appears to be a simplified and summarized ritual to invite the spirits and offer them temporary bodies. All the necessary steps for the ritual are taken. First, the client is interviewed by the facilitator, and the facilitator mentions who will be represented: "We'll need your mother, father and sisters." or "Choose your father, uncle and your son.". This is the first time the names of the ones who are invited are spoken out loud. Next, the client chooses representatives from the participants in the seminar. Again, they use spoken words: "May I take you as my mother?", "Would you stand in the place of my father?", "Do you want to be my aunt?". Shamanic tradition teaches that such simple questions can be heard by spirits and souls, and they have the power to invite them in. Further, such questions dedicate the body of a representative as a temporary body to a specific soul. When, during this phase of the constellation process, a client invites the representatives in a light and casual way, most facilitators will stop him. If the client does not feel the weight of what he asks, both the facilitator and the one chosen to be a representative immediately sense that something is disturbed. From a shamanic point of view this is logical. The voice of the client has to carry an invitation to the world of spirit, and only when a person is grounded and composed will his voice have strength and power. Before choosing representatives, the client was interviewed by the facilitator, and the life and fate of various family members have been described. Knowing the spirits are only voice distance away, it is easy to imagine that the souls and spirits belonging to a particular family are somehow activated, triggered, awakened by such an interview. In fact, there are cultures in which the names and lives of the dead are never mentioned; just mentioning their name might already draw them near. So, when the client asks a representative to 'be' a certain family member, the spirit or soul of that person can hear this and knows he is welcome. He finds there is a body waiting for him: a representative, receptive and attentive. The representative's body serves as an anchor point for the spirit. Information becomes available. Such symbiotic states of consciousness are typical of shamanic practice. The souls of the shaman and his helping spirits often merge; they become one for the duration of the ritual.

A representative in a constellation may represent someone who is alive or someone who has died. The representative experiences no difference between them, it is just as easy (or hard) to represent someone who is alive as someone who is dead. The soul of a dead person has no body, it exists just like a spirit, but the soul of a living person is anchored in a physical body. That raises the question whether, when someone is represented who is alive, his soul would somehow step out of its physical body in order to link up with the body of the representative. Experience shows that an individual who is represented in a constellation does not notice anything unusual or specific during the time he or she is represented. There is no detectable 'movement' of the soul in the sense of a soul jumping from one body to the next and back. To understand this, I can build on the image of the radio I gave earlier. Radio waves have all kinds of frequencies – high and low. Still, they all travel through the same medium: 'ether'. This medium permeates and supports all the different waves, no matter what their frequencies are. The relationship between temporary bodies or vehicles of the soul and the soul itself could be compared to the various frequencies and ether. 'Soul' is somehow able to permeate more frequencies at the same time, so when a representative represents a living person, both are in contact with the same soul.

In the following chapter, I will explore a traditional shamanic image of the soul and see how this can further stimulate our thoughts about the constellation process.

8. The Multiple Soul

The first time I was introduced to the concept of the soul, or souls, being able to move in and out of the body was during the first time I supported a Native American medicine man during his work and travels for a few weeks, many years ago. Never before had I had the opportunity to study with a spiritual teacher in a more private context. I was still inexperienced in many ways, and to my growing surprise, in all the four weeks we were travelling, I did not hear a single direct instruction or explanation about spiritual techniques. My teacher had been seeing groups of people and individuals, we had been doing ceremonies and visiting people's homes, but somehow when I looked back at what was said and discussed, I could find no practical tips or descriptions of shamanic techniques whatsoever. I still had to get used to the fact that medicine people only rarely give explanations and instructions. I was also unaware at that time that there are many Native Americans who strongly resent that their medicine people teach non-Natives, no matter what the context might be. A spiritual teacher who gives direct instructions on traditional spiritual matters may be subject to gossip, exclusion, and even direct violence.

Only at the very end of that month did I finally get something that could be considered a direct instruction in ritual work. My teacher advised me to daily perform some small ritual gestures which included the use of water, and I was told that this was for the benefit of my soul, so it would be fed and would stay around. I cannot describe the details of this small ritual here because it was specifically given for my personal use only. I was intrigued by the idea of the soul being able to come and go and needing to be kept in good condition. How could the soul not be in good condition? My concept of the soul, as far as I had one, was static. I thought my soul was the spiritual part of myself that was forever present and always healthy. How could my soul not be in my body, wandering around on it's own? I had never even thought of the possibility of a soul drifting off. I thought the only time a soul would step out of a physical body would be the moment of death. After being introduced to the idea that the soul is able to travel around, and even needs food and care, I started to pay attention to what other teachers and the various shamanic traditions had to say about these matters; I soon found out that there was a whole world of ideas about the soul.

Studying the many shamanic concepts and theories about the soul in detail only makes sense when the context of traditional healing practices is taken into account. There is one basic concept or model however that is also interesting within the context of systemic work: the concept of multiple souls from the Siberian traditions. Most shamans of Siberia and Mongolia believe that humans have not just one single soul, but at least three, four, or even five – the exact number varies in different traditions. What I present here is only a fragmented and very basic summary, based on the general ideas about the multiple souls that are shared by many shamanic peoples.

The multiple souls occupy different positions in and around the physical body, and each has a different nature. Usually, one of them is closely interwoven with the physical structure; it is specifically connected to the bones and, according to some traditions, also to the nails and hair. This soul resides in the body at all times. It is thought to carry animalistic power and vitality, and sometimes it is also seen as the cornerstone of individual consciousness. The various traditions have different opinions about the soul that carries the foundation of individuality; it all depends on how many souls there are thought to be in total. When the first animalistic soul is not considered to have individualized personal consciousness, usually it will then be said that there is an extra soul residing in the physical body that carries the basic individual characteristics that make up the awareness of a self. So, one or two souls reside constantly in the physical body, linked to the autonomous vital strength of the body and the sense of individuality. The other souls are positioned outside of the physical body, either close by or far away from it. Usually, one soul is described that lives very close to the physical body but not actually in it, and at least one other soul that lives in the wilderness of nature or in the world of spirit. There may also be more souls of the last type, for example one that lives in the lower world and one that can be found in the upper world. All the souls are connected to specific aspects of human experience. One will have for example spiritual wisdom; another then has the practical knowledge that is necessary for day to day survival. Together, the multiple souls embody all human qualities and characteristics, both of practical and spiritual nature, either in manifested form or in a potential state. Traditional shamans use their models of the multiple souls to diagnose and treat illness. When someone is ill, each soul is checked separately, because a disease may originate in just one of the souls. Are all the souls in good health, are they weak, are they polluted with foreign energies? Has one of them wandered off too far and is now lost somewhere?

A shaman will always check whether all the souls are still present when someone does not feel well. According to the Siberian traditions, all the separate souls are able to move around. Souls will for example easily wander off at night while their owner sleeps. Their return causes dreams. The form and content of a dream depend on where the souls have been and what they have experienced. Sometimes a soul may wander off and not return, not wishing to come back because it has lost interest in what is going on in its owner's life. It is also possible that a soul leaves because it is forced to do so by external circumstances. Serious physical accidents can for for example, simply force a soul out of the physical body, or a shock can break the links between the body and a soul that lives close to it. In these circumstances, souls will very soon get disoriented and lost. A further observation, made in traditional shamanic context, is that a soul may be stolen by spirits, or by shamans who want to create trouble.

The shamanic traditions say that the single or dual soul that is strongly connected to our bones and physical body cannot leave the body for very long; it would result in death quite soon. Of the other souls, at least one usually stays very near the physical body or its owner. The other souls however spend their time in nature or in the other worlds, and these souls can disappear without it being directly noticed. In fact, it is hard to be aware of these souls themselves, even if they are near. According to tradition, we can normally only feel the positive effects of the souls' presence, or the negative results when they are gone and disconnected from us – but not the soul itself. Noticing or feeling the absence of one of the mobile souls can be compared with feeling the effect of switching the heating off in a big room. When it is comfortably warm and someone switches the heater off without your knowledge of it, it takes quite some time before you realize that something has happened. In the beginning, the temperature goes down so lightly that you do not notice it at all. Then, you may start to feel only slightly chilly but you do not consciously register it. Only after a longer time do you get a bit cold and you start to think about the heater. The same goes for the absence of the mobile souls. When one of the souls leaves, it is not immediately noticed. Only when a soul is gone for a longer time does its owner start to feel that something has changed. Maybe he will experience some vague discomfort, or a certain lack of energy. Maybe he gradually starts to feel depressed or loses interest in the world around him. Negative effects connected to soul loss are noticed relatively soon when one of the souls that stay close to the physical body has left, then it may only take some hours or a few days. However, when one of the souls that only sometimes visit their owner in his sleep and habitually live in the other world has left, it may take many days and even weeks before someone starts to notice the effects of losing it.

There is something peculiar concerning the presence of the various souls: we get used to having them around, or to not having them around. It might for example, be that for someone, seen from a model of five souls, three souls are present, one is only half connected and one is totally gone. When you ask him how he is doing, he will probably say: 'Okay!'. Whatever the habitual, 'normal' situation is concerning the presence of the various souls will automatically become someone's frame of reference; whatever is the status quo during a longer period will be experienced as normal. So, regardless of whether someone says he feels all right, his own feelings do not always indicate how many of his souls are generally present. That is why, in classical shamanic practice, whenever someone visits a shaman to ask for help or healing, the shaman will check whether all the souls are present. When, after a check, the shaman finds one of the souls missing, he will, in a trance, send out one of his own souls to check the spirit worlds for the presence of the lost soul. When he finds it he brings it back, and then reconnects the lost soul to the client's physical body. When the souls are all in their right places, the patient notices a difference, and will realize he did not really feel so well before the healing. The presence of the souls does not create spectacular blissful feelings or intense spiritual experiences; it simply supports a subtle calmness, a sense of health and inner balance, a relaxed kind of curiosity about the world and other people.

The model of the multiple souls that are able to move shines an interesting light on the processes at work during constellations. One of the questions that comes up easily in systemic work is how a representative can feel and know so much about the person he represents, and about the family that person belongs to. If a person has a number of souls that can move around at will to a smaller or larger degree, one of these souls could theoretically join the constellation and somehow merge with the souls of the representative. A soul, connected to a physical body or not, will pick up an invitation as soon as it is spoken with respect, as explained earlier. It is not hard to imagine that when a constellation is set up, some souls will notice this even if they are very far away, and they may come over to check out what is happening. It should be considered here that according to tradition, all the different souls, except perhaps the one connected to the bones of the physical body, have a separate individual awareness. At the same time, they are part of their owner's life. When an individual has been suffering from illness or hardship, all his souls will individually feel the need for healing and support. The soul that finds a constellation and representative waiting for it will most likely recognize the context as an opportunity for healing, release, or resolution. Since the souls that are most mobile are the ones whose departure is only noticed after some hours, days or even weeks, theoretically any given soul can easily join a constellation and return to where it came from without any effect on its owner.

According to tradition, most souls that have completely lost contact with their owners are not able to return on their own. Not that there would be a technological problem that makes it hard for them to return – souls that have wandered off far are simply slightly or completely disoriented, and do not even think of the possibility of going back. When a soul has left because conditions in its owner's life were too hard for it, or because of some injury or accident, it simply forgets whom it belongs to. A lost soul will continue to exist on some kind of automatic pilot, without any initiative of its own.

It often happens that the disease or problem that made the soul leave has been healed or solved for a long time, but the soul still does not return. Traditionally, it is the task of the shaman to make contact with such lost souls. The shaman will communicate with them so they become aware again of who they are and where they belong. Lost souls will respond easily to help that is offered them, and they can quickly be restored to awareness. It is not hard to imagine that a family constellation may have a similar effect on lost souls as shamanic soul retrieval. A lost soul may be drawn in while a constellation is set up. It then links up with the representative, and experiences the healing movements of the constellation process. When the constellation is finished, the soul leaves. During the constellation, it has found new balance and regained its vitality; it has a clearer sense of whom it belongs to. If a trauma was the reason for its departure, it is likely that during the constellation, at least a part of the trauma has been processed and healed. Instead of continuing to aimlessly wander around in the spirit world, the soul will remember its history clearly and is probably now interested in returning to its owner – at least if that owner is still alive. When the lost soul of a dead person has been represented, after the constellation, that soul may go to that part of the spirit world where the souls of dead people live.

The Siberian model of the multiple souls describes how various souls can easily go here and there. Normally, the movements of these souls are not detectable for their owners. The image of mobile souls may possibly explain how representatives in a constellation know what is going on in the family they represent as soon as they are all set up. Each representative knows instantly how he relates to the others; he does not have to wait for these feelings to develop, there is no process of sorting out information. For the representatives in a constellation and the audience watching them, it is clear that 'something' has come in, and this something, from a shamanic point of view, could be some of the mobile multiple souls. The movements of souls and spirits are unimaginably fast. Existing in the other worlds, made up of energy vibrating on various frequencies, the souls or spirits do not have to travel through our physical world when they want to appear in a ritual or constellation. Space and distance mean something different for them than for us. The frequencies of the other worlds permeate the physical world everywhere, and so they can easily show up everywhere. When they are invited during a ceremony, they attune to the voice and person that invited them, and if they feel interested in joining, they will connect and make themselves felt. When they feel like leaving, or when the ritual, or a constellation, is finished, they retreat again.

Occasionally, during shamanic rituals, the spirits or souls will leave suddenly before the ceremony is ended, and something like this can sometimes be observed during a constellation too. In some constellations the energy just drops away all of a sudden. A constellation that was developing well may lose something, and from that point on, no intervention of the facilitator can bring back the power that was first there. Something seems to have truly left; a quality is suddenly gone. When a constellation loses its power, the energy of the audience starts to disperse as well, people start yawning and looking at their watches. Such sudden shifts can usually be traced to a remark or even just the attitude of one of the representatives. A constellation in progress is constantly influenced by the representative; what they say, feel and do may strengthen the process or weaken it. When the life drops out of a constellation, the shift is sometimes caused by the client who has replaced his own representative and now stands in his own place. A client is sometimes unable to accept the healing movement that is developing and manages to break off the process. One little sentence, a gesture or remark which is completely out of tune with the difficult and delicate movements of the soul, and for all the representatives in the constellation it feels as if the plug has been pulled out. The sudden loss that is felt at these moments could well be the result of the present souls and spirits retreating. In shamanic ritual, the spirits sometimes leave when one of the altars is disturbed, or when someone interferes with the healing movement by singing a song that is not appropriate for that part of the ceremony. When that happens, the whole ceremony, or at least the phase in which the disturbance took place, has to start again. Often the spirits will return, but not always. When in a constellation a healing movement is consciously or unconsciously disrupted by the client, it may sometimes be resumed if the client is taken out of the constellation and a representative takes his place. It also happens that a constellation loses power without interference from the client or another individual. The facilitator will then probably say something like 'I feel we have no permission to do the work'; it is then felt that some intelligence does not support the constellation. There may for example, be a family secret that is too heavily guarded to make a healing movement possible. In such cases, the energy may feel very dense and unclear, and then it is felt that something is working against a discovery. But it may also be that there is no more energy available, and in that case, the souls or spirits may have left.

There is a further aspect of the multiple souls theory that is interesting in the context of the family constellations. Some Siberian cultures, but not all, describe that among the various souls that every individual has, there is a personal soul and a family soul. These two souls both 'record' what happens in their owner's life, but after physical death, they will separate from each other. According to most Siberian traditions, the souls live on after death. So, both the personal and the family soul live on. The fate of the individual soul may be reincarnation or not, but someone's family soul will reincarnate in the same family. If a family has died out, the family souls who used to reincarnate in it again and again will then reincarnate in a family that resembles the family from which the souls originate. A family soul is shared by a limited number of individuals as they are born as members of the successive generations, and it carries all kinds of memories from within the family. Not all memories, since a given family soul can only be connected to one person at a time. As the years go by, the family soul continues to incarnate in successive generations in the family tree. When a certain man dies, his personal soul may incarnate in another culture, but his family soul will reincarnate in his own family, for example in his nephew. When this nephew dies, the family soul he had will incarnate in another family member of a next generation, for example in his own granddaughter. After the granddaughter has died, it may go to her brother's daughter. The family soul moves through the generations, from one lineage to the other within the same family system. Each family member also has an individual personal soul, and this may very well be a reincarnated soul too, and it can come from anywhere: from another culture, country, or continent. The family soul however always comes out of the family. The two souls are separate entities and follow their own programs independently of each other, for better or for worse. Sometimes someone's personal soul and family soul have many conflicting interests or impulses, causing a difficult life, filled with frustration.

The shamanic cultures' concepts about the soul are based on interpretations of observations the shamans have made over many generations. Obviously, people saw the behavior patterns and inclinations of deceased family members return in newborn family members. The image of a family soul reincarnating in the family is a logical image within the context of the shamanic traditional world view and spiritual cosmology. The image of a family soul is also interesting in the context of systemic work; it could clarify some of the dynamics that create certain types of trans-generational entanglements within families. The image of a reincarnating family soul would help to understand the dynamics involved when a certain fate suddenly returns after some generations, when there is no possibility of someone copying a personally known relative's fate out of unconscious loyalty. In an earlier chapter, I gave the example of a mother and daughter whose lives got mixed up because of their unconscious attempts to support each other. Such dynamics can be understood relatively easily: mother and daughter know each other very well. But what can we say of a grandson who commits suicide at the same day and in the same way as his great-grandfather whom he never met – not even being aware of the fact that his great-grandfather had killed himself? The idea of a family soul being transmitted from one to the other within the same family could be relevant here. It would explain how some very specific fates can be repeated so literally. The idea of a family soul residing in a single individual also helps to explain why normally just one person picks up the fate of a certain family member while all the others in the family go free.

The family soul is an interesting concept in many ways. When you look at systemic entanglements that are related to homosexuality and transsexuality, the image of the family soul makes sense too. Often, when a homosexual or transsexual client sets up a family constellation, it is found that one of the dynamics operating in the family is that the client, in his own family, had to represent somebody of the opposite gender. Sometimes, in constellations, cross-gender entanglements are found for heterosexual people as well, and there are also same sex identifications for homosexual and transsexual people. So, from the constellations, no final conclusion can be drawn that a cross-gender entanglement would be the actual cause of homosexuality or transsexuality; it is simply observed that this specific type of entanglement often coincides with it. In some shamanic cultures, specifically the ones from the high Arctic, when a child is born, the shamans will try to trace the origin of its family soul. The newborn child is seen as the reincarnation of a deceased relative, and the child will get the dead man's or woman's name. It will keep this name until puberty. A boy may have a feminine family soul and a girl may have a masculine family soul, and so a boy may get a woman's name and a girl may get a man's name. At puberty, the child will receive a new name, one that fits their physical sex. Many will take the new name and identify with it, but some will not. Most traditional shamanic cultures, both in Siberia and North America, state that besides man and woman, there are two other genders: a man-woman in a male body, and a man-woman in a female body. The people of these third and fourth genders are seen as intrinsically different to men and women, since they are not only masculine or feminine, in their soul they are both. In most shamanic cultures, the people of the third and fourth gender had specific spiritual responsibilities; in the Siberian cultures many of them became shamans.

Taking images out of a certain culture and using them to explain the dynamics we sense in constellations and entanglements is risky, no matter how inspiring it may be. The exploration I have made here should therefore just be seen as an experimental train of thought, and suggestions of possible answers I found should not be taken as definite conclusions. The Siberian model of multiple souls can be of help in some ways, but thinking back on the earlier chapter in which I explained that a soul needs a temporary body to make itself known, it also raises new questions. If the soul itself cannot be felt or noticed by our senses, what about the multiple souls mentioned in Siberian shamanism? Are they actually souls, or are they temporary bodies? In the next chapter, I will move on to another model to explore the nature of the relationship between the soul and temporary bodies in more depth.

9. The Soul, the Four Bodies, and the Personality

Over the years, I have studied with different shamanic teachers, but also exchanged information and experiences with teachers and practitioners of other spiritual traditions and schools. What I found useful I have integrated into my work, and some of the terminology and concepts I use in the description of the next model are not originally used in shamanic traditions. Still, it was during many years of shamanic practice that the next model of the soul, the four bodies, and the personality was formed and refined.

The starting point of my description of this model is the soul. During meditation, shamanic trance, or other spiritual practices we can have a direct experience of our own soul. The soul is however much greater than what people are able to experience inside themselves. The soul is limitless. Through spiritual discipline, someone can learn to perceive more and more of the soul, but the personal limits always continue to determine the scope of perception. The soul itself is not limited; the soul is the vital energy that permeates all living beings. Students of many yogic and Buddhist schools constantly strive for the actual experience of the totality of the soul, most often called enlightenment or self-realization. In traditional shamanic practice, this type of direct experience of the total soul is never actively sought, although that truly advanced shamanic practitioners experience it spontaneously from time to time. Every individual's own soul is the door to this greater oneness. From the most individualized personal aspects of the soul to the great whole, essentially the soul is one. We can say that we all have individual souls, but on some level, those individual souls are one too.

Besides a soul, each individual has four bodies. These bodies are each of a different nature and consist of different substances; they are called the physical, ethereal, astral, and mental bodies. The

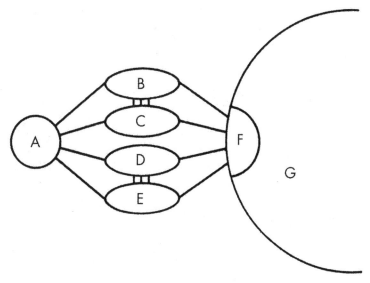

A = Personality
B = Physical Body
C = Etheral Body
D = Astral Body
E = Mental Body
F = Individual Aspect of Soul, or Personal Soul
G = Greater Soul

physical body is the anchor for the other three: the ethereal, astral and mental bodies permeate the physical structure, and necessarily also each other. The four bodies exist in the same space on different vibrational frequencies. They are interwoven and constantly influence each other. However, at the same time, they continue to be separate entities that can be experienced by our consciousness as separate and independent structures. The four bodies are each connected to the soul and receive strength and life from it; each body is in fact a separate vehicle for the soul.

The physical body consists of bones, blood, tissue, and other gross matter. The ethereal body is next in line. It is only slightly bigger than the physical structure. The ethereal or energetic body is the vehicle for the life force that vitalizes our physical body. In a way, it is a more subtle version of the physical body, and the two are completely interwoven. In acupuncture, the concept of meridians is used to describe discernible flows of subtle electromagnetic energy along lines that connect various organs and body parts. These are the flows of the ethereal energy, vitalizing the physical body. Just as the first two bodies are closely interwoven and form a kind of unit, so the third and fourth body function as one whole. The third body is the astral body, which is of a more subtle nature than the ethereal and physical bodies. Usually, it is perceived as a field that is much wider than the physical structure. Sometimes it is described as a body of flowing and vivid colors, with seven wheels placed on positions on the spinal column: the chakras. Only very few shamanic traditions have described a phenomenon like chakras, and since I have been trained in shamanism, I do not use the concept of chakras in my shamanic practices. The astral body, whatever its exact form, is the vehicle in which the images of memories are stored. Besides that, it is the body that feels emotions. A third important quality of the astral body is mythical consciousness: dreams and symbols are its language. The mental body, which is the fourth in line, is the body of structure. Just like the different parts of the physical body are connected through the 'wiring' of the ethereal body, so the mental body provides the astral body with a subtle underlying structure. For many people, the word mental is associated with the capacity to think, but thinking is not only related to the mental body. The mental body is best described as the structure that makes thinking possible. Imagine that your thoughts are a spider, running along the lines in a web. The patterns in the web determine how the spider can walk, or how thoughts develop. The mental body is not the spider; the web: it is a structure that influences the movements of thought, but without guiding the thoughts actively. Just like the ethereal body vitalizes the physical body and upholds it with structures and energy patterns, so the mental body is closely interwoven with the astral body. It consists of pathways and structures that determine the course of dreams, associations, and thoughts. The ability to think however, is a capacity of the personality, which is an entity of a very different nature than the soul and the four bodies.

When you take a moment to sit down with your eyes closed, it is easy to experience the workings of the four bodies. As you sit, you can feel the weight of your body on the chair, you sense the warmth of your hands and feet, and can feel the moisture in your mouth. You can also feel the ethereal energy that subtly vibrates in your body, the life force in your bones, muscle, and skin. Images and memories that originate in the astral body run through your mind, accompanied by associative thinking that automatically follows the patterns and structure of the mental body.

Each of the four bodies independently has sensations that then blend together into a single cohesive experience in our awareness. It is the personality that makes this possible. The personality filters the output and sensations of the four bodies and allows what it judges as important to rise to the surface of awareness: information which flows in from four different sources becomes part of a single stream of attention. This inner unified reality that is composed of information of the four bodies determines how we relate to the world around us. Our personality determines what we experience as reality; it interprets the events and the world around us.

The personality manages awareness, and occasionally will direct all its attention to one of the bodies only instead of filtering and mixing the sensations of all four into one whole. It will usually only do this when one of the bodies is extremely active or agitated, and is going through very intense experiences. Imagine for example running ten kilometers. After a certain amount of time, awareness solely focuses on the physical body. You feel the movements of the muscles, you are hardly thinking anymore, you do not even think about whether you should stop running or continue. There is no emotion, no fantasy or story in your mind anymore. Your awareness of the physical body is much more acute than usual; in a sense you have totally become the body now. In the same way, the personality can direct all attention to one of the other bodies. During some meditation practices in which the physical body is kept motionless for long stretches of time, one may become aware of the ethereal body of energy. When awareness has shifted from the physical body to the ethereal, consciousness just experiences a vibrational field in which it is impossible to discriminate between the various parts of the physical body. The experience of the ethereal body changes the experiences of inner space: there is no way to discriminate between the space between two fingers or the space between the top of the head and the soles of the feet; the experience of physical size does not exist in the ethereal body. Everything feels either very big or very small, and sometimes it is not even possible to differentiate between these two concepts anymore. One simple exercise that, for many people, leads to an experience of the ethereal body, is the extreme slow movement of one of the arms. If you want to do it, sit down in a relaxed position and close your eyes. Put your right hand on your knee. Then practise moving your hand to your left shoulder, something that takes about one or one and a half seconds. Now put your hand on your knee, and again move your hand from your knee to your shoulder, but take at least an hour for this single movement. The movement has to be so slow that you cannot even determine whether you are actually moving or not – still, the *intention* to move your arm is there all the time. Many people who do this exercise experience all kinds of changes in the way they perceive their arm, and finally it cannot be felt anymore at all. What is experienced is simply a field of energy. Often, not just the sensation of the arm changes: the whole body awareness shifts into the unfamiliar sensations of the ethereal body.

Attention can also be shifted to the astral body completely; this happens for example during some hypnotic trances. Someone who is hypnotized can totally withdraw into an inner world of memory, image, and myth, and completely lose sense of the physical body and its material environment. The familiar sensation of daydreaming also signifies that attention is retreating into the astral body. You can for example, 'wake up' to your physical environment after having been lost in thoughts and images, finding yourself with a book in your hands that you had been reading, waiting for the traffic lights to turn green, or standing at the window looking at the garden. Finally, awareness can also be shifted to an experience of the mental body, but this is hard to describe. When awareness is completely focused on it, it is immersed in a world of abstract patterns, context without content, which is hard to put into words. Such an experience is quite rare, and is usually only had by people who have been trained in spiritual practices of concentration for a long time, or it accidentally happens to those who are under the influence of powerful drugs.

The descriptions of the four bodies can, to a certain extent, be superimposed on the shamanic concept of the multiple souls. Both the four bodies and the multiple souls make up the totality of human experience in latent and manifested form. The ethereal body can easily be compared with the soul that vitalizes the physical body;

both the first soul and the ethereal body are closely connected to the physical structure. When awareness is anchored on this first soul or ethereal body, there is a clear and strong sense of self, although this feeling is not accompanied by individual characteristics. The model of multiple souls describes now the animalistic soul or souls are practically one with the physical body, as the ethereal body is. The next soul is not actually in, but still very close to the physical body – in fact, it is often depicted as living on the physical skin. The astral body, which is the next in line after the ethereal, is bigger than the physical-ethereal structure, and so seems to hover around it, and thus we have the image of a field of color around physical substance. This resembles the image of a soul enveloping the physical body. The next soul is usually seen as an entity living in another world, visiting only in dreams. The mental body basically occupies the same space as the astral, and so also surrounds and permeates the physical body. Maybe the mental body and the soul that is far away could be compared in the sense that the actual experience of the mental body is hard to achieve and cannot really be translated into the words we use for the description of more familiar experiences. In that sense, the mental body is certainly otherworldly. The astral and mental bodies are in many ways like the more mobile souls. In the model of the multiple souls, the sense of the past and the future are carried by two different souls. Looking at the bodies, you find that the astral body carries memory, while the mental body has the capacity to make planning possible. Not all aspects of the multiple souls correspond however to the model of the four bodies. The soul that brings dreams for example, should be one of the souls that lives very far away and just occasionally visits. In the model of the four bodies just described, this imore likely to be recognized as a faculty of the personalized part of the one greater soul, or as an effect of the travels of the astral body.

There is one aspect of the theory of multiple souls that is hard to transfer to the model of the four bodies, and that is the idea that one of the multiple souls carries a part of the family memories and another one carries just personal experiences. As far as I have been able to determine, the four bodies, the personality, and the soul each have their own ways of storing experiences, turning in them in various types of memories. The soul keeps an original experience contained like a static image or field, it does not change it. The personality will tell stories about past events: it filters and directs attention radically, shying away from painful memories and embracing positive ones. The astral body carries what we usually call memories, but these are actually images that are created anew all the time, images based on past events, reshaped according to the personality's new insights and opinions. The physical, ethereal and mental bodies do not store experiences in the form of actual memories. They simply react to a powerful experience with a change of form – patterns and conduits of energy may change; they may for example open up or become blocked. The physical, ethereal and mental bodies may also store experiences and information in the same static way the soul does. For example, ten years after you hurt your knee, a healing massage may still release pain; something was obviously stored in the tissue. Each of the four bodies, soul, and personality may get wounded and scarred in their own particular way. Based on these observations, the shamanic image of multiple souls incarnating in and out of a certain family brings up a general question about reincarnation. Does the soul reincarnate, or do the ethereal, astral, and mental bodies reincarnate? And if one or more of them should reincarnate – would they be able to carry their stored experiences and memories with them into their next life? What about personal memories and family memories? In the next chapter, *The presence of the dead*, I will look at the theme of reincarnation again, for now I will continue with the exploration of the four bodies.

According to the traditional shamanic model of multiple souls, the different souls are all mobile, even the one soul that is closely interwoven with the physical structure is able to move to a certain extent. The various souls' capacity to move away and get lost in the other world is seen as an important factor in the development of disease. The four bodies are also mobile, although I observed that their movements are subtler and smaller than those described for the multiple souls: the subtle bodies do not get lost in other worlds. Still, even the relatively subtle movements the ethereal, astral, and mental bodies make in relation to the physical body can easily cause discomfort and can also be a cause in the development of chronic disease. Once, at the start of a seminar, a young man arrived with a cut on his hand that was bleeding. When I asked him what had happened, he told me that a car had hit the front wheel of his bike and he had fallen on the street. Apart from the cut in his hand, which was not deep, he had no injury, but he still felt a bit in shock. I started the seminar by introducing the group to the concept of the four bodies, and explained something about the tendency of the subtle bodies to get displaced after sudden physical trauma. I took a rattle in my hands and sang for a while to bring myself into a light trance, and in that state I checked the position of the young man's ethereal, astral, and mental bodies. I saw that his ethereal body was positioned slightly backwards and upwards; it was in fact only partially overlapping with his physical body. To me it looked as if his ethereal head was looking at me over his right shoulder, in itself a funny sight. Using a shamanic technique, I grasped the ethereal body and simply clicked it back into place. My 'client' looked around for a few moments and seemed amazed. His reaction impressed the other participants in the seminar: "That feels good! The colors are more bright – I haven't seen clear colors like this for a long time. And everything is sharp again – it's like a mist is gone or something!" From this reaction, I understood that the displacement of the ethereal body I had corrected was not caused by the bicycle accident at all; it was a chronic condition that must have existed for a long time, otherwise my 'client' would not have been so surprised at the results of my work. Strange as it seems, when one of the bodies has shifted out of position, after a while we hardly notice the effects of this shift anymore. Feeling chronically incomplete because of a shift in the position of the bodies can become synonymous with feeling okay after a while, simply because the negative effects are not that dramatic to the senses and have usually built up only gradually. A healing ceremony that restores the bodies to their correct positions can then have an effect as if somebody cleans windows that have collected months of dust and dirt. When all the bodies are in place and interacting well, things seem clear again; not just the auditory and visionary perception, but also thinking itself.

The shamanic term 'soul loss' is only truly functional within a traditional shamanic context, and therefore I do not normally use it myself. Yes, I have seen how displacements of the ethereal, astral, or mental body can create a range of troubles from minor discomfort to serious chronic disease. However, I have never personally met someone who had lost one or all of his complete ethereal, astral, and mental bodies, except for someone who had been in a coma for a long time. An ethereal, astral, or mental body can be in very poor condition, and sometimes it is so weak that it is hardly present; but according to my experience some part of it is always still there. I have listened carefully, and when traditional shamans say that they have to go and look for a specific soul in the other world, they do not specifically state that the soul has totally left. This leaves room for the possibility that some of the higher souls are able to split themselves into various parts, which may then individually get lost in the other world – and this is something that I have often observed with regard to the astral body. According to my personal experience, a permanent displacement or a poor condition of one or more of the four bodies can create similar effects to traditional shamanic soul loss, without that body first having to be completely disconnected and lost in the other world. Even in the traditional description, someone who suffers from soul loss will still partially keep his ability to remember things or think of the future, it is not the case that certain functions of the four bodies are suddenly gone completely. Even if certain processes of the bodies are less vital than usual, the processes in themselves remain reasonably intact. This also indicates that traditional soul loss does not mean complete loss of one of the higher bodies.

The four bodies serve as vehicles for energy and presence of the soul. When one of the bodies is displaced or in poor shape, it can fulfil only a part of that particular function, and a person will lack a corresponding quantity or quality of the strength and guidance that originate from the soul. From that perspective, the term soul loss is accurate when the bodies are displaced. Typical results of diminished presence of the soul in the four bodies can be, among others, losing interest in life, feeling disconnected from others, thinking obsessively or repeating images of certain troublesome memories, losing sight of the overall structure of one's life, feeling disoriented, and finally depression.

Checking the position and condition of the four bodies has proven to be a useful tool in shamanic work in many circumstances for me and the people I have trained. Using the model of the souls, the four bodies, and the personality, one can learn many things about the origin and treatment of illnesses, including some types of mental illness. The four bodies influence the personality; this has the task of making sense of the experiences and activities of the four bodies and uniting them in a coherent experience of reality. I have sometimes found that somebody can appear to be thoroughly mentally handicapped, while in fact the personality in itself is essentially still able to function perfectly well. In such cases, there is a disturbance in one of the bodies, and the personality just cannot make sense of it anymore; the whole experience of reality changes accordingly. In such cases, shamanic healing by a skilful and experienced practitioner will be appropriate and effective even for people diagnosed as schizophrenic or psychotic. Mental illness can however also be caused in the personality itself, and the four bodies can each still be in quite good condition. When this is the case, treatment should be left to a psychiatrist or psychotherapist, a shamanic ritual would probably only confuse the client more.

The four bodies influence the personality, but there is a flow in the opposite direction too. The personality, in its turn, also influences the four bodies. It directs thinking and determines what is important or possible in any given context. It makes choices that have a direct effect on the condition of the bodies. For example, as someone is swimming, the physical body gets tired and signals that it is time to stop and take a break. The personality can choose to ignore this signal because it wants to train the body to become stronger. The swimmer continues swimming, and the physical body gets trained and gradually learns to swim longer and longer without the need for a break. The astral body can be trained too. In a restaurant, somebody sees a photo on a magazine and has a very disturbing association connected to personal memories. The astral body reacts and sets off an emotional cascade. The personality can stop this process; it decides for example that it is not appropriate to cry out loud in a restaurant, and so it will exercise control, forcing the astral body to learn the skill of holding an emotion without diving deeply into it. The interactions between the four bodies and the soul also go two ways. The soul helps to shape the four bodies and strengthens them. But at the same time, the experiences of the four bodies have an influence on the soul and help it to develop.

An important aspect of the model of the soul, the four bodies, and the personality, is that the soul and the personality are out of each other's direct reach. If you visualize their relationship in terms of space, the four bodies are standing in between them, making direct interaction impossible. Soul and personality are two different and separate fields. As I said in an earlier chapter, the personality's habitual thinking has no access to the experience of timelessness, an inner experience of the soul. The soul and the personality are therefore hardly aware of each other, but at the same time, they are continuously confronted with each other's strengths and weaknesses through the four bodies. The soul and the personality can however gradually learn to attune to each other, and even finally shake hands. This only becomes possible when the four bodies are completely purified through spiritual practice. Then, the soul can shine through them with ever-increasing strength, and the personality attunes more and more to the soul's knowledge and power. When the four bodies are in a purified condition, they are no longer an obstruction in the communication between the soul and the personality, but a conduit. The personality has to be trained to be more receptive of the soul; it must learn to maintain the inner experience of silence the soul needs to make itself felt. Through prayer, the personality can create structures of thinking that invite the soul to come very near. Soul and personality will always be separate, but they are able to learn to function very closely together.

10. The Presence of the Dead

During the last few years, in circles of people involved in the development of systemic work in Germany, the question has been raised whether the dead, represented in family constellations, can find healing in the same way as the living do. This question has all kinds of responses and many discussions have followed. Some people are happy that the issue has been addressed – for them it is obvious that the dead are in some way still alive and will actually benefit from the constellations. Other people feel that the dead are not really alive anymore as independent souls; they see the dead in constellations simply as aspects of the client's own soul. For them, the dead are gone, but they continue to exist in the memories their loved ones keep of them, and when a person finds healing for himself, so too do these parts of him because they are integrated in his soul. Again, other people feel very uncomfortable with the discussion, because looking into these matters could be interpreted as acknowledgement of the family constellations as a spiritual phenomenon, while they instead feel it should only be classified as a therapeutic method. For these people, the discussion about healing the dead leads to a dangerous mystification of systemic work. There is no way that a discussion among people with such different opinions can lead to any kind of clarity. The precise question in itself – can the dead find healing through a constellation – is not even truly relevant, since it is only an expression of a clash between different views on reality. The various points of view are accompanied by deeply felt emotions, and are sometimes vigorously defended by people who are actively participating in the discussion. If you experience and define yourself as a single being, basically independent and unique, separate from others and free to choose your own life and destiny, then one of the consequences is that the dead are out of reach, lost and gone. And not only the dead, but the living too, even if this is not immediately evident. If you experience and define yourself as not just participating in life, but actually as being part of a greater force that unites you with others, the question of whether the dead can be healed is irrelevant. How could the dead, who are felt to be close, be denied their healing? The danger of a discussion about the nature of the dead is that it can very easily develop into an ordinary fight about who is right and who is wrong.

I have observed that many people involved in the discussion have limited experience with the actual presence of the dead in their work. Clearly, most have a lot of experience in their own professional fields; some may for example be very good therapists. The therapeutic language is however by its very nature not the right medium to explore the possibility of the dead's ability to receive healing. In psychotherapeutic language, the dead only exist as a presence of memories, a presence that contains no true life of its own even if it affects the living. The people whose experience with the dead is limited to seeing representatives of dead people in family constellations will necessarily have a limited perception of them, since they can only compare the appearance of the dead in a certain constellation to their appearance in other constellations. The family constellations may teach us various important things, but they cannot lead to final conclusions about the nature of the dead's ability to heal. Other observations than those that can be made in family constellations should be taken into account before any conclusions about the dead's ability to heal can be drawn: the dead can manifest themselves in many ways.

I want to explore the spiritual dimensions of family constellations by looking at them from the shamanic perspective, and so I want to look specifically at what the shaman's observations of the dead are. What I present here is partly based on traditional shamanic knowledge (translated into images and concepts that fit our western way of thinking) and on the observations I have made as a shamanic practitioner. I will start by looking at the process of dying, because this automatically leads to a description of the condition of the dead. Over time, generations of shamans and medicine men have made detailed and careful descriptions of the dying process. When a trained shamanic practitioner is in a trance, his awareness can be withdrawn in the more subtle bodies, the vehicles of the soul, and the process of dying can be observed quite precisely from the various perspectives of the ethereal, astral, and mental realms.

As I explained in the previous chapter, every individual has four bodies: a physical, ethereal, astral, and a mental body. The soul strengthens each of them and exchanges information with the bodies, so both the soul and the four bodies are continuously influenced by each other. The personality is the guardian and director of awareness, and the personality and the four bodies influence each other too. During the process of dying, the soul, the four bodies, and the personality are each affected in different ways. The first thing that happens when somebody dies is that the physical body stops functioning and a process of decay starts: it rapidly falls apart. When the ethereal, astral, and mental bodies get disconnected from the physical body, the personality withdraws from the physical body too. After physical death, the ethereal, astral, and mental bodies and the personality are now left without physical anchor, and gradually lose connection with the physical world. A few days after the death of the physical body, the ethereal body also starts to fall apart. The ethereal body has been so closely interwoven with the physical body that it cannot maintain its structure without it. Most often, the astral and mental bodies disconnect from the deteriorating ethereal body around three days after physical death, but when someone has been trained in spiritual practices to strengthen the ethereal body, this may happen at a later moment, easily up to a week or more. When the astral and mental bodies are freed from the ethereal structure, they can theoretically start to withdraw into the spirit worlds, which are of an astral-mental nature.

What has to be considered here is that together with the astral and mental bodies, the personality is basically still intact. The personality is a medium that is connected to each of the four bodies. With the physical and ethereal bodies gone, the personality has obviously become a more limited structure than it was – but it is still functioning. However, when the impulses of the astral and mental bodies are not tempered and balanced anymore by the heavier, slower physical and ethereal bodies, the personality will start to react to its environment in much the same way as the living know from their dreams at night. During dreams, the links between the astral and mental bodies on the one side, and the physical and ethereal bodies on the other, are temporarily weakened. As a result, very little critical awareness is left, and associations and emotional impulses rule the personality. After physical death, someone can get lost very easily in this dreamlike state, caught up by the impulsive and intense reactions of his astral body to whatever it encounters. In this state, with a personality of limited scope, someone can live on for a long time in his astral and mental bodies, easily for many years. If someone, during his physical life, has learned how to become the manager of his emotions instead of being ruled by them, he will benefit enormously from this now. There are many shamanic and Tibetan Buddhist practices that aim specifically at gaining control over awareness in sleep, during dreams. This, next to learning to rule over emotions without suppressing them, is seen as one of the best possible preparations for death. The astral and mental bodies will finally gradually weaken and lose substance, and as they fall apart, the personality also dissolves. The individual part of the soul is left without a vehicle, and it automatically retreats completely into the greater soul. In a way, it has never been truly separate.

Small aspects of the greater soul continuously connect to unborn children that are growing in the womb of their mothers. Whether this phenomenon should be defined as reincarnation is a matter of perspective. The soul itself is not the personality, so when reincarnation is defined as the return of a real 'self', the process of the soul reaching out to a fetus in the womb cannot be called reincarnation. The personality dissolved when the astral and mental bodies finally lost structure, and that particular sense of 'I' will never be reborn. Still, something of an individual's life is carried by the smaller soul that has retreated into the greater soul. The soul does not carry the astral body's thousands of anecdotes, images, and memories that the personality cherishes, but it keeps something of an overall picture, a flavor, without details. The smaller soul has changed as a result of being connected to four bodies for a lifetime; it has certain characteristics now that it did not have before. Some of its intrinsic tendencies may be strengthened or weakened, certain qualities may have developed. However, although these are individual traits, they do not create the particular sense of self that is characteristic of the personality. The soul is part of something great and does not know any boundaries, whereas the personality is separate from everything around it. When a new child is born, it has a complete physical and ethereal body; the astral and mental bodies are there too, but they are still fluid and have little structure. All the four bodies constantly exchange information with the soul. Since the personality is formed in the interaction between the four bodies and their environment, through its influence on the four bodies, the soul will have an indirect influence on the formation of the child's personality. The soul may carry both positive and negative tendencies, so its gifts for the child can be for better or for worse. There are cases where a soul connects to an unborn child while it is still clothed in a weakened astral and mental body. In that case, it should be expected that the 'former life' will have some kind of direct influence on the formation of the new personality of the child. Various spiritual traditions have different opinions about why and how often this phenomenon takes place, and few of them agree with each other. It seems to me that there are many possibilities; apparently the soul has a variety of ways to incarnate.

The soul itself has individual characteristics, but at the same time it continues to be part of something greater. True separation and individuality exist only on the levels of the physical body and the personality; the boundaries between the more subtle bodies and their environment are less strictly defined. After death, the astral and mental bodies continue to be vehicles for the individualized soul, but the personality imposes fewer boundaries on the soul since it has partially dissolved. The soul is less restricted, and it will expand its awareness to some extent. After physical and ethereal death, the first zone of the greater soul that makes itself known in the individual soul is the area that, in systemic work, is sometimes called the family soul. From a shamanic perspective, the term family soul is too limited though, since not only family members are included in the soul's expansion. After death, an individual's soul also opens up for the souls of people that have been close to him during his life, such as the life partner and good friends. When someone who dies had a specific passion or hobby that had a strong influence on the way he led his life, even unknown people who shared that same passion will be included in the soul's expansion. However, even if the term 'family soul' is too restricted, since I am looking at what is relevant for the family constellations, I will continue to use it. So, after death, the smaller soul expands and feels in itself the family soul, the presence of others. This extended awareness motivates the deceased individual to move into the actual presence of those other souls. Ideally, after death, the soul is drawn specifically to those people that died earlier and are already at peace in the spirit world.

After death, most of the dead retreat deep into the astral world; they move into the zones where those who died before them are residing. Ideally, the attention of the newly dead turns away from the living. In this state, they can continue to live on for many years, until their astral and mental vehicles and their personality finally dissolve. Their souls can then retreat completely into the greater soul. The dead may however also continue to have an interest in their loved ones who are still alive. Many people who die continue to be loosely directed towards the living for some years. They do retreat into the other world but will occasionally drop by in the dreams of the living, for example to tell them that things are fine with them, or because they want to give support. Sometimes, when the dead are burdened, they may ask attention for the things that they could not resolve during their lives in the physical world. There are also some individuals who, after death, do not travel into the other worlds at all. They continue to hang around on the borders of the astral reality, their attention fixed on the physical world, often on their family and friends or – if they made any – on their enemies and victims. People who died because of an accident, as a victim of violence, or under narcosis in a hospital sometimes stay attuned to the physical world because they simply have not noticed that they died. As I explained earlier, the personality of those who live on in their astral and mental bodies is partly gone, and individuals in that state do not think as clearly or logically as people who are physically alive. One of the characteristics of behavior in dreams at night is that people seldom draw conclusions when something strange is going on. They just respond to something unusual as if it were normal. Dreaming is much like the state that souls are in after death; they may be vaguely aware that something unusual is going on but they do not draw any conclusions from this.

From the shamanic perspective on the relationship between the dead and the living, it is best if the dead retreat into their own world. They should not be encouraged to stay around. Their work here is over, and continuing to focus on the physical world will lead to frustration. Even if the dead move into the spirit world, both the dead and their loved ones continue to be connected. Via the soul, the living and the dead continue to be in contact. If the spirits that are connected to us are happy, we will feel their joy as strength and support in our own soul. If they are unhappy, we will be somewhat restless and agitated. The same goes the other way; if we are unhappy it casts a shadow in the world of spirit, but our joy will be felt in their souls too, and it will give them strength to face the challenges that are part of their existence. So, even though the dead should retreat into their own world, we still carry some responsibility for their wellbeing and they still carry some responsibility for ours.

It is one of the most common tasks in shamanic work to help people who are not aware that they have already died, or those who do not dare or wish to turn away from the physical world. This task is performed regularly by all traditional practitioners. Dead people who are still wandering around in their astral vehicles are fairly easily noticed by a trained shaman, who will attempt to communicate with them and see how they can be helped to move on to the next world. Many shamans have become shamans only because as children they had the natural ability to see the dead who were still around. It can very easily be verified whether the child really sees the dead because experienced shamans can see them too. To test whether a child has true visions of the spirits, a shaman will sometimes interview the child when the dead are around to find out what it sees exactly. When the child's perception is good, it will later receive the training to become a shaman. One can also become a shaman after a near death experience. When someone is very ill and is on the very edge of death, the soul partly disconnects from the physical and ethereal bodies and starts to withdraw into the spirit world. Because the connection with the physical world has become so weak, the soul, clothed in the astral and mental bodies, retreats further than is normally possible. Someone who has consciously gone so deep into the other world will come back a changed person, his perspective on reality has shifted. While he was deep in the other world, he may have been noticed by the spirits that live there, and on returning to the world of the living, a helper spirit may have followed him. Knowing how to come back from the world of the dead, accompanied by a spirit helper, he then has the necessary qualifications to help the recently deceased move over, and he will be taught by a shaman how to make use of his assets.

Somebody who wants to become a facilitator of constellations does not need to experience a near death experience or have a special talent to see the dead. From one perspective, that is very good, because in that way many more people can help the dead than just those who can actually communicate with them in their astral bodies. From a traditional shamanic perspective however, it is not necessarily always so good, because it is not just the healing effect of the constellation that supports the dead. The attitude of the shaman or facilitator also has a direct influence on them: it is not just the constellation but also the facilitator that determines whether the dead find healing. Since the dead have lost part of their personality, most of them are, in a specific way, not so strong. Even after a healing, they may still get lost again, or succumb to sadness and loss. A shaman knows this, and after helping the dead through a ritual, he will continue to think of them in a specific way. For some time after the healing ceremony, the shaman will not just think of the dead in the sense of remembering them, but by focusing his own thoughts a shaman will help the dead to keep their minds focused and strong. One of the best ways to help the dead is to regularly visualize them with their personality functioning well, with a clear and strong sense of determination and purpose, their thoughts concentrated and joyful. The dead will absorb these images and they will find it easier to remember who they are because of them. Such positive images serve as a mirror for them; they are strengthened by them. When the shaman who helped the dead continues to think about them in this way, the dead will continue to remember what their task is; to travel into the other world.

When someone is leading a constellation, and in this way helps to find a resolution for the representatives of the dead, that is a good thing. When after the constellation he continues to think of the dead with respect, and puts the final images of the healing movement in the timelessness of his own soul, that is even better. However, when a facilitator, after a constellation, tells himself that the dead do not really exist and therefore cannot be healed, he is, from a shamanic point of view, seriously weakening the effect of the healing movements of the constellation. Not only for the dead, but also for the other people who were represented and the client. And finally, also for his own soul.

11. The Soul and the Constellation Process

Throughout the various chapters I have already looked at many aspects of the constellation process, exploring possible answers to some of its unexplained dynamics. Now I would like to look, step by step, at the energetic processes at work during the constellation process in its totality. However, before starting the description of the various phases of the constellation process, I will briefly summarize the images and concepts about the soul and the spirits that have been explored until now.

I started with the concept of timelessness. Inside ourselves, we can find a timeless quality that also has the quality of an inner space. This experience of timelessness is just out of reach of the personality: when consciousness is focused on timelessness, the habitual structures of thinking have little power or temporarily dissolve. I see this awareness as an experience of our own soul; one of the individualized aspects of the greater soul that we are part of. Then, I explained how other souls and the spirits need to be clothed in a temporary body in order to manifest themselves to our senses. We can feel our own soul inside ourselves in the silence of timelessness, but we can only perceive a spirit or soul outside of ourselves when it is clothed in some kind of vehicle. I used the image of radio waves, vibrating on certain frequencies, as an illustration for vehicles employed by the soul. The soul is then seen as the ether in which the frequencies exist; in its pure state, the soul is not seen or heard by us. After this, I explored various aspects of the traditional shamanic model of multiple souls. All of an individual's different souls carry different qualities and are able to move around, except the one(s) responsible for vitalizing the physical structure. I described the traditional ideas about soul loss, when one of the souls has drifted off to the world of spirit and loses contact with its owner. Next, I introduced the model of one soul, the physical, ethereal, astral, and mental bodies and the personality. Both the soul and the personality are in continuous interaction with the four bodies, influencing them and in their turn being influenced by them. I explored how the traditional concept of soul loss relates to the four bodies, and concluded that soul loss would mean a displacement of the subtle bodies in relation to the physical structure, or loss of energy of the higher bodies; specifically loss of parts of the astral body. Then, I described how during the process of dying, the physical and ethereal bodies disintegrate while the astral and mental bodies continue to be vehicles for the individual soul for some time. The personality of the deceased loses part of its structure with the loss of the physical and ethereal bodies, and as a result, the soul includes in its sense of 'I' an increased awareness of the presence of loved ones, both alive and dead. There is still a strong sense of individuality, but others are felt to be present, nearer. Finally, I mentioned how this inner awareness of others motivates people who have died to move into the spirit world, or, contrarily, keeps them partially or totally focused on the physical world. The shaman is the one who communicates with those deceased that continue to be pulled close to the world of the living, and he tries to help them to move into the spirit worlds.

SETTING UP A CONSTELLATION

After the client has been interviewed, the facilitator chooses which family members need to be represented and asks the client to choose representatives. Often, at the start of a seminar, a facilitator will say it does not matter who are chosen to be the representatives. This is true in many cases, but not all. There are constellations where one or two people who are represented prove to be key figures in the process of making the healing movement for the whole family; most of the facilitator's attention is focused on them. Often, these members of the represented family had an exceptionally hard fate and carried a heavier burden than other members of the family, or it may be that they had to close their hearts completely in order not to feel personal guilt or other pain, or something else which was serious was going on in their lives. In my experience, it really does matter who is chosen as a representative for a key role in a constellation. I have regularly heard that after a constellation, the people who were chosen as such key representatives said something like: "I was absolutely certain that I was going to be chosen to represent this person as soon as the client stood up to make his choice!", or "I just knew it was going to be me." The client, while choosing, sometimes knows that he can only ask a certain participant in the seminar for a specific representation. Often, only when the constellation is finished does it become clear what made the representative the right one for the specific task of representing a certain person. Sometimes, the representative has in his own life already resolved the issues the person he represents has to face, and so he has already developed the specific strength needed to bring the constellation to completion. The opposite may also be true; it sometimes happens that a certain healing movement is needed not just for the one who is represented, but also for the representative. It may for example happen that a certain participant in a seminar has never been able to accept the strength and love of his partner. Being chosen to represent someone who needs to accept the love of his partner gives the representative the opportunity to go through the process himself, and later benefit from it in his own life.

The client, looking around to find the right representatives, has to be in a collected state. In that state, in contact with his own soul, the greater soul can direct him during the process of choosing. The personality has no direct access to the guidance of the soul, so thinking while choosing is usually not helpful. The client simply tries to feel who is the right person for a certain role. I remember once setting up my family constellation in a seminar with about twenty participants. When I was choosing representatives I checked the circle, looked everybody in the eye, and waited till something from inside responded. Mostly the response I felt was not very clear and strong, and it did not seem to matter much whom I chose. However when I had to choose my fifth representative, one of the participants suddenly was literally bathed in light as I looked at her, as if somebody had put a spotlight on her. I realized with surprise that I had no memory at all of looking into her eyes when I was choosing the earlier representatives. It felt to me that my soul had made me first overlook her so she would still be available to represent a certain member of my family that turned out to be the key figure in the constellation.

Having chosen the representatives, the client now has to actually set up the constellation: each representative needs to be given a place that feels right to the client. Someone in a collected state will put up his constellation without much agitation, even when during the interview with the facilitator just moments earlier strong emotions arose. A collected client can sense where the representatives have to stand he does not need to think about it. He guides the representatives to their places, possibly taking a short break now and then to check the responses in his own physical body as he moves the representative. Where does the client find the information he needs so that he can find the right place for the representatives? Obviously not in his personality; the instruction of the facilitator is always clear: "Do not think about where to put them. Forget your ideas of what your family looks like, who is close to whom and so on. Just open up and feel where they have to be." The physical body seems to be able to indicate when a place is right or wrong, but that body in itself can not be the actual source of knowing, it lacks the specific type of intelligence needed to position representatives for family members in a group room one by one. The physical body is however one of the four vehicles for the client's own soul. It is likely that the client's soul actually guides the process of setting up the constellation, making itself felt through sensations of the physical body. Maybe it is not even just the client's soul, it may very well be the family soul that was mentioned earlier. The community that is made up of our family and friends is very close to us on a soul level, and an individual soul needs to open up only a little bit to find access to these parts of the greater whole. When the personality of the client is in a concentrated and collected state, it leaves the physical body free for impulses from the soul level, and the client can simply follow these impulses.

When a client has put up his constellation and the representatives are in position, in almost every case the representatives immediately have information available. They do not need time to adjust themselves. The group of representatives forms a physical vehicle for the patterns that are felt in the soul of the client. Representatives have used all kinds of words to describe what they felt as a constellation was set up: 'Something descended.', 'Something clicked in.', 'Something filled up the space.' or 'It was there, I just knew.'. The question is: what or who descended, clicked in, filled the space or was there?

Is a representative temporarily linked with one of the souls of the shamanic multiple soul model, or is he fused with the astral body of the one he represents? This is a possibility, but experience suggests it is not likely. A trained individual can merge his astral body with the astral body of somebody else and receive information that way; this is done in certain traditional shamanic practices to communicate with specific types of spirits. A merging of the astral bodies however has a very distinct quality and feel to it, and from the typical responses of representatives in constellations, it can be deduced that they are not just tapping into an astral energy. The astral body is always preoccupied with the images it creates and the stories it tells which are based on memories; it is in constant motion, and it is always looking for emotional content. Very few people's astral bodies are able to hold on to a silent image for long, since the astral body has little patience with the felt essence that exists outside of linear time. In constellations, the representatives seldom or never have the impulse to make up associative stories; they just embody suspended feelings, based on the felt essence of the relationships they sense they have with the other representatives in the constellation. They know and feel with a timeless quality. Representatives are for example, able to stare each other in the face for minutes at a time without distraction and agitation, simply feeling the depth of a single quality of love, hate, or discomfort. This timeless quality is characteristic of the energy of the soul itself, and not of the astral body. However, even though the representatives do not merge with the astral bodies of those they represent, occasionally spirits or souls in astral bodies do show up during constellations. Usually, they want to find healing. I earlier described a constellation in which I saw the spirit of a drowned man, standing in between the representatives. Most of the times I have seen a spirit in a constellation it concerned someone who was not represented, but it has also happened that I have seen someone's spirit or soul standing next to the person representing him. At those moments I have not observed any exchange on astral levels between the two: the representative is obviously perfectly able to access useful information from somewhere else other than the astral level. All these observations together lead to the conclusion that it is not the astral body of the one who is represented that has entered the representative's field of knowledge. To me, it is logical to assume that in the constellations the soul is expressing itself through the four bodies of the representatives, including the physical body.

The responses of representatives show that their information originates in the soul. But which soul – thinking back on the Siberian model – the client's individual soul or the client's family soul? Or even the representative's soul? These questions may be interesting, but in the end they are superficial, because the soul makes no real distinction between the self and the other. Even within the context of the soul having smaller and greater aspects, it is still one. One can say that the individual, smaller aspect of the soul would not have access to all the feelings of the family, so what is felt in a constellation would have to originate from a part of the soul that is greater than just the individual aspect of it. On a soul level, the client who is setting up his constellation opens up for the family soul that he can experience within himself. At the same time, the representative who is set up in a constellation reaches out too, opening up for the one he represents. There is no actual movement of the soul here in the same sense that, for example, a physical body can reach out to another body. The link between the various aspects of the soul is made in the dimension of the soul itself, outside of place and time. The 'other' is found within, in the representative's own soul, and an influence coming from the soul is felt in the representative's four bodies. The representative can then describe what he experiences. When a representative has to represent an abstract concept like death, Switzerland, or lust for life, the dynamics are actually much the same. Mankind's thinking creates structures in the greater field of the soul. These structures are strengthened over generations; gradually the image starts to be an independent field with distinct individual characteristics. Abstract concepts will eventually become conscious, individualized aspects of the greater soul. As spirits, they are able to manifest themselves in temporary bodies; either in an astral vehicle during a shamanic ritual, or in the four bodies of someone who represents them in a constellation. The entry door for all those who are represented – the living, the dead, and the abstract forces – is the inner soul of the representative.

During a Constellation

When a constellation has been set up, the facilitator will carefully observe the representatives. He may ask how they are doing, sometimes he may withdraw to let the representatives follow their impulses and see how they move about. Sooner or later it will be clear to him what the dynamics in the family are, and when specific negative or disruptive patterns are evident, the search for a resolution starts. During this process, whatever the outcome is, the representatives speak and act in the name of someone else, linked to the other's soul. Often, there is also a representative who stands in the place of the client who has set up the constellation, but it also may happen that the facilitator asks the client to stand in his own place after placing the other representatives.

Each individual has fixed ways of doing things, and it is very hard to break even the smallest patterns. For example, people who always bake their omelet in oil will usually feel very disturbed if they have to use butter. If you always use a black pen to write your letters, it feels unpleasant to have to use a green one. With emotional and rational patterns, it is even more difficult to step out of a routine. A person in need of healing can only act and think along the old patterns that his four bodies and personality provide. Sometimes healing is possible within this limited structure, but just as often it is not. When the possibilities for resolution within these fixed patterns are not sufficient to resolve a problem or to heal a psychological wound, the soul will start to suffer. It will continue to try to provide strength and guidance, but if these cannot be accepted or interpreted within the fixed patterns in the four bodies, they cannot be integrated. After some time, the soul will give up and wither away; it contracts and shies away from the wound or problem. In such conditions, a soul can find a new impulse to support the healing when it is represented during a constellation. Different people never share exactly the same problems and patterns: each individual reacts differently to stress, grief, pain, and other difficulties. When a soul, in a constellation, can make use of the four bodies and personality of a representative, it is offered a new set of structures in thinking and reacting. The soul will sense this and again send out a healing impulse. Unhindered by the specific limits and blocks of its owner's four bodies, it will expand again.

When the soul is free of its owner's physical and ethereal bodies, it is more free and fluid. However, it will also be less able to develop. One thing that has been observed by many spiritual traditions, including shamanism, is that a soul that is free of a physical-ethereal structure can change its patterns only very gradually. It is the same for the souls of the dead who are permanently disconnected from a physical body, a soul that has temporarily loosened the connection from the physical structure during a dream, or for a part of the soul that may be lost according to the classical definition of soul loss. It is simply necessary for a soul to be in a physical body in order to be able to make some changes and develop, or at least: to do this fast. The physical body, because it is rigid and dense, acts like a mould for the soul, directing the soul's experience to a certain extent, forcing it into a certain shape. 'Shape' is a symbolic word here, since the soul has no actual shape. Still, the soul is imprinted deeply by the physical structure. A soul without a physical body, and that needs to make a shift in awareness, or must learn to see things in a different way, can be helped best by connecting it, welcoming it in a temporary body. Physical bodies are perfectly suited to this task.

In traditional shamanic practice, various techniques have been developed through which, souls that need healing are temporarily connected to a physical body to get their 'treatment'. Siberian shamans who went to look for lost souls or the souls of the dead, would put those souls in their costume after having found them. The shaman's costume is an exteriorized structure of the shaman's body, functioning at the same time as a spiritual map of the universe. For example, the depicted vertebras and ribs of the shaman's skeleton symbolize the stem and branches of the cosmic world tree. On many shamans' costumes, there are special metal hangers that serve as the temporary vehicles for lost souls and the souls of the dead. By placing the found souls on these hangers, the shaman incorporated the soul in his costume and in himself, he in fact absorbs them into his own soul. The souls stay in the hangers for the duration of the ceremony and hear all the prayers and songs, and thus receive the healing. The constellations are in fact a variation on this familiar and old theme: the representative's physical body is the temporary body for the soul of the one who needs healing.

During the constellation, the representative has opened up his own soul for the individual he represents. The soul of the one who is represented starts to work through the soul of the representative. In essence they are one, but it is just as easy to depict them as two individual streams of consciousness: during a constellation both souls will experience and express themselves through the four bodies and personality of the representative. The representative's four bodies will give the other's soul new possibilities for expansion, for release and change. Seeing the four bodies as mechanical devices, one could say that the representative's tubes, conduits, and software are different than those of the four bodies of the represented person. The patterns in the four bodies of the representative will mould the soul of the represented in a new way, so the soul will experience certain new restrictions, but also new opportunities for expansion and release. At the same time, the representative will also be changed. When someone has been set up to represent another person during a constellation, his breathing changes, the muscle tone changes, his posture changes, the amount of available energy changes. The representative's four bodies adjust to the essence that is carried by the other's soul. However, that adjustment can only go so far, since the representative's own soul is still 'occupying' his own body too, next to the soul of the represented person. And so, during the constellation process, there is a continuous dynamic process of mixing and adjusting of soul and energetic structures. When asked, or spontaneously when he is distracted or provoked, a representative can switch back to the perception of his usual self, but just as easily he can open up for the other's soul input and adjust to that again.

It is the ability to switch between the two different patterns of the soul that makes healing possible in a constellation. If a representative were completely 'taken over' by the other's soul, if the patterns in the four bodies of the representative were completely overruled by the other soul, then there would be no difference between represented and representative anymore. No sudden shift of the soul could be expected. And if the representative were to remain himself completely, and continue to feel only the contents of his individual smaller soul, he would not have access to any knowledge of the other, and he could not himself be touched and changed inside. Only when a representative allows both aspects of the greater soul, that of the represented and that of himself, to work through his four bodies at the same time, does healing become possible. Understanding this precise dynamics of the soul, the healing process gains a subtle beauty. The representative's own soul gives strength and structure when a difficult healing sentence needs to be spoken. Imagine a father has never dared to look his dead child in the eyes. Now, while he is represented through the soul of the representative, he has the courage to actually do this, and says: "Now, my dear child, I see you." The father's soul benefits from the representative's strength; it helps him to do what must be done. When the representative and represented work together in this way, you can see the healing movement sink in and anchor itself in the greater soul. During and after speaking healing sentences that facilitate true resolutions, the facial expression of the representative undergoes a series of changes; muscles contract and relax, all the available energy moves and changes when the healing sentences are doing their work in the patterns of the soul of the represented and the representative. For me, these are the most fascinating moments of a constellation; the dance of the two souls in one physical body, the one helping the other, making use of the same mind and energetic structures.

Sometimes, the constellation process does not lead to a resolution. There may be several reasons for this. The soul of the client may not be capable or willing to open up for some specific healing movements, and then the representatives have difficulty getting access to the greater soul. The family soul may not permit certain things to be looked at directly because they are too painful or too burdensome for the family members. Then there is simply no way the constellation will unfold and lead to healing. It may also be that the constellation cannot be guided towards balance because certain important information is missing. That information in itself does not have to be a hidden secret at all. In each family, there are events and stories that are simply not transferred to the next generations. Unless someone of a younger generation asks a direct question that brings such information up, it gets lost when the older generations die. When information is missing, it is important to respect the fact that in a constellation, factual information cannot be retrieved, because the soul does not carry actual memories. The soul of the represented person has no access to the facts of history at all; it is only imprinted with the *effects* of history. The soul embodies timeless essence, not stories. When it is clear that essential information is lacking in a constellation, the facilitator can therefore only try to find out more by interviewing the client, and should refrain from asking the representatives about their feelings or opinions about the historical facts of the people they represent. Finally, a constellation may also get stuck because the soul of a key representative refuses healing. Although this is very rare, it does sometimes happen. When a constellation gets stuck because of this, the facilitator may have difficulty recognizing that it is actually the representative that refuses the healing movement instead of the family soul that is represented. When in doubt, the only possibility for a solution would be to change representatives, and then it is immediately clear who was unable to move; the represented individual or the representative. All the reasons why a constellation would stop developing in a healing direction that I have mentioned here are based on the idea that the facilitator is capable of doing his work, can attune himself to the systemic energy field and understands the dynamices and possibilities of the constellation process. If the facilitator does not have enough experience, many of his constellations will have only little power and limited effect.

Ending a Constellation

A constellation is ended when a healing movement has been completed, or a decision has been made to stop the constellation without such a completion. If the client has not yet taken his own place in the constellation process, during this last phase, usually the client's representative is asked to make way for him. Standing in his own place, the client feels the effect of the changes in the constellation, he may be asked to say a sentence or two. Finally, the facilitator says: "Get out of your roles." All the representatives step out of the constellation, return to their seats, and focus their awareness on their familiar sense of self again. The facilitator may ask the client to sit next to him for a while, and may point out some things that he finds important, or he may make some psychotherapeutical interventions. Finally, the client also retreats to his seat.

12. Effects of Constellations

Some constellations are followed by a good or even miraculous development: the client feels he has found his place, health problems dissolve, family members who did not communicate for years call each other and make appointments to have tea together. However, just as often there is no immediate tangible result, no clear shift, change, or healing. Many factors influence a constellation and the process that follows afterwards, so many that it is always impossible to predict what the final results will be. However, several of these factors can be recognized, and their description enhances understanding of the dynamics that are at work after a constellation.

When a client has set up a constellation, he witnesses every movement the representatives make, and hears every sentence that is spoken. The constellation affects the client's soul and personality, and both of these integrate the experience in a different way. The effect on the personality is immediate and clear. Many clients are happy with their constellation; the dynamics that unfolded have given them new insight into their family, and their own position within it. Although it is hard to understand immediately all that a constellation has brought to light, for most people a constellation brings relief and clarity. When a constellation has ended, the facilitator will often talk to the client for some minutes. He may want to explain certain dynamics that became visible during the constellation process. The strange thing is that some clients simply cannot truly grasp what is said at such moments. While all those who were representatives and even the whole audience will understand exactly what the facilitator points out, the client himself cannot grasp what has happened and what is explained. The majority of clients set up a constellation because of a problem they have had for many years, and this means they have also thought about this problem for all that time. They will have certain theories about the root of the problem, and about the ways it could be resolved. More often than not, the constellation process shows a dynamic that is completely unexpected, sometimes even contrary to what the client has always thought.

I remember a constellation that was set up by a man whose parents had divorced when he himself was very young. The father had left his wife and children, and although the children hardly knew their father, they had always despised him for this. The constellation showed that the father himself had not wanted to leave the family at all, but that he had left in the mother's place. The mother was actually the one who wanted to leave and be free, undoubtedly because of entanglements within her own family of origin. The father managed to prevent her from abandoning the children by leaving himself. All of a sudden, his departure proved to be an act of deep loyalty towards his children; he wanted to make sure they would continue to be taken care of by their mother! This was a hard one to swallow for the client. Furthermore, the constellation showed that the hatred the client had always felt for his father was actually a feeling that he had taken over from his mother, who was unconsciously outraged that she was prevented from abandoning the family. While the mother was unable to express this anger since it would expose her as selfish, the son had unconsciously expressed it for her. This constellation was of course extremely disruptive for the client. He had always thought of his father as a monster, and of his mother as an innocent victim, and confronted with the constellation, he found his assumptions about the family's history seriously challenged. In the talk I had with him about the constellation, he saw no other alternative than to reject it. Accepting it would have meant too serious a threat to his habitual view on reality. It is not strange that a client's personality cannot always make such enormous leaps of perspective graciously after just a few minutes of discussion with the facilitator. Everybody else in the seminar can accept what the constellation has shown with ease, because they do not have the energetic patterns and belief structures of the client; on the personality level, they do not identify with the story. If the client could easily incorporate the hidden dynamics that were visible in the constellation in his belief system, he would probably have found healing at an earlier point in his life.

Some facilitators interpret a client's inability to accept a constellation as resistance, and then try to deal with them as if the client is undergoing a psychotherapeutic session. I personally feel that the therapeutic concept of resistance is usually not very helpful in such cases. The client is not unwilling to change, but his behavior originates in fixed old structures of the personality and the four bodies, structures that are truly unable to make a sudden change. Most constellations are initially disruptive for the client, because the process shows dynamics that are going on in the soul, where the personality has never had direct access. Even when the information that a constellation has brought to light is felt to be true, and the healing movement has brought relief for the client, his personality will still need time to adjust and integrate the soul's view of reality. From the shamanic point of view, it is best to allow the client to feel and absorb only that which he takes in naturally and easily, and to do little or nothing more. That does not mean that the facilitator should not actively guide the client to find a way to relate to the work that has just been done, and find a balance with it; it simply means that a client who cannot immediately take it all in should be respected. When I spoke to the client whose constellation I just described, I suggested that he allow himself to reject the constellation, but I also asked him to remember the various movements of the representatives from time to time. After a few months, he told me that although he did not believe that the story that had come to light was true in every aspect, he looked at his father now with more respect. The blind hatred he had always felt for his father had dissolved.

Can trans-generational entanglements of fate be healed through a family constellation? Often a constellation shows that the client or another member of his family is actually representing or repeating the fate of someone else, someone who lived before or is still alive, and has been excluded from the family in one way or another. Is it the child who has chosen to stand in for the older one, or has the older one somehow been able to actively recruit a child to represent him in the family? Souls are connected, and on levels that cannot normally be experienced by the personality, every soul is part of the greater whole. There is however no actual personal involvement in the mechanisms that make a certain child's soul connect to another family member whose fate needs to be acknowledged. It seems to be the greater family soul itself that creates these connections. Even an unborn child's soul can already hold the patterns of the soul of someone else who needs to be acknowledged in the family, and these patterns will have an influence on the shape of the child's four bodies, and the personality that forms in childhood. Later, in adulthood, the patterns of the other who needed to be represented will have become an integral part of himself. When a family constellation brings such a situation to light, and releases the soul from the original entanglement, the soul will, from that moment on, be freer to develop new patterns. The effect of the old patterns will however continue to be felt to a certain extent, because they are fully integrated in the four bodies and the personality. Healing does not mean return to the situation before the entanglement was there, healing simply means there are some additional options.

Systemic work is witnessed by the client, but the family members who have been represented have themselves not seen the constellation set up and unfold. As described in the previous chapter, during the constellation, their souls were influencing the perception of the representatives. The family members were connected with the process in this way, but on the levels of the personality and the four bodies they have not been touched directly by what has happened. However, after a constellation, the individual soul of everybody who was represented will be shaped differently to a greater or lesser degree. And, after a constellation, the soul of a person who was represented will automatically have an influence on its four bodies; the new strength it has found and the new patterns that have been experienced or even imprinted during the constellation will have some effect. The four bodies may resist this influence or they may yield to it, they may fight it or they may welcome it. It may take them some time to adjust, or they will somehow react immediately.

When a soul was linked to the four bodies and personality of a representative during a constellation, it temporarily experienced another way of responding and acting. If it was a healing experience, and the soul has gained strength, it will automatically transfer this experience into the various structures of its own four bodies. It is actually not an active transference; it is more that the soul will try to hold on to its new shape. The four bodies may resist this because they automatically want to hold on to their familiar old shape. After a period of mutual adaptation and adjustment, the soul and the four bodies find a new balance together. Sometimes the new patterns of the soul were strong enough to imprint the four bodies deeply; sometimes only a part or even just a tiny fragment of them could be integrated. Then, yet another step has to be taken because now the personality has to adjust to the change in the four bodies. The same process of adjusting will take place, finally resulting in a new balance between bodies and personality. Understanding this long and gradual process, it becomes logical that the majority of constellations will often only have a subtle effect on the members of the client's represented family members. For those who were represented without witnessing the constellation themselves, an immediate dramatic healing or a complete change of strategy of the personality can only sometimes be observed. Although miracles happen, the most likely result is a subtle shift in certain habitual patterns of thinking or feeling. That little opening is more than enough though; it can develop over time if the person wants it to. After a constellation, the soul knows an alternative to earlier strategies, and it is free to choose.

When a dead person has been represented, the effects of a constellation are more direct. An individual who has died has left behind his physical and ethereal bodies, and so the new patterns of his soul that have been created during the constellation have only to work through the astral and mental bodies to become part of the personality. These two bodies are less dense and rigid than the physical and ethereal bodies and offer less resistance, and so the soul will usually be able to keep the constellation's effect intact to a greater extent. The personality of a person who has died may be more erratic and less structured than the personality of the living, but in the context of the effect of systemic work, this is an advantage. A personality that is less rigid is more open to change and to new impulses that come, via the astral and mental bodies, from the soul.

Sometimes the movement that was possible in a constellation can, for technical reasons, not have a practical result on the concrete daily lives of the ones who have been represented. This is often the case when it concerns people who are mentally handicapped from birth, or who have gone truly insane. Some mental illnesses develop because of a wound or scar in one of the subtle bodies; the finer energetic structures can be handicapped just like the physical body. Such a handicap of the subtle bodies may be the result of a birth defect, a disease, or an accident. Someone's soul may be essentially healthy, but when the four bodies can only offer a severely limited structure, they do not allow a normal growth or function of the personality. Someone in such a situation cannot interact freely with his environment, but in a constellation, his soul has a chance to temporarily 'use' a fully functional set of healthy bodies and personality. Sometimes the soul has been so limited by the dysfunctional four bodies that is not immediately able to use this opportunity; it continues to act from the limits that its own four bodies have imposed upon it. The representative will feel crazy. However, the souls of some mentally handicapped people will blossom when they are represented, and reach out to the representatives of the ones they love with a pure gesture that is out of their reach in daily life. Such an opportunity is very valuable, since it releases tensions in the soul and the family, but it cannot lead to any change in the represented individual's daily life. The structural damage in the four bodies that have caused the handicap cannot change; the new strength the soul has found during the constellation has no direct effect on this. Apart from helping the soul temporarily during the moment of the constellation, constellations in which mentally handicapped family members are represented can create a very powerful healing image for the client. Imagine a child that has become a 'living vegetable' through brain damage as the result of an accident. This girl is now being represented in a constellation that has been set up by her parents. The representative of the child can speak to the representatives of the parents and express what needs to be expressed. The three are at least for once able to hold and comfort each other. The constellation will make a deep healing movement possible for the souls of both parents and child, but it is unlikely that the constellation will result in the child waking from its coma. Or, imagine a father who has gone completely insane many years after the war, because his personality could no longer contain the horrors he had to suffer as a soldier. His children have only known him as a very violent and dangerous man, who was finally secured in the closed ward of a mental hospital. The father's soul can still love his children unconditionally, and when the father's representative can express this love just once in a constellation, free of madness, it can heal many wounds in both the father's and children's soul. It would not be realistic to expect that after the constellation the father would be sane again, only rarely will a constellation result in seriously insane people regaining mental health. A constellation like the ones I have just described should simply be kept as a healing image in the client's soul, without an expectation of an improvement in the outer circumstances. When a constellation is respectfully kept alive in this way, much inner strength can come from it.

Constellations do not only have an effect on the client and his family, but on the representatives too. When a representative stands in for someone else, he experiences a shift in himself for the duration of the constellation. Sometimes this shift will be subtle, and at other times powerful. The represented soul has a specific perception of reality, and for the duration of the constellation, the presence of this other soul automatically opens up certain unused channels in the four bodies of the representative. Representatives describe all kinds of clear physical sensations during a constellation – and just as the physical body is affected by the soul of the one who is represented, so are the subtle bodies. Imagine the soul's energy as electricity, which is moving through certain wiring in the four bodies. Some wires and conduits are always full of electricity; others receive just a tiny bit or even nothing. Now, during representation, the representative's soul has opened up for another soul, and the energy of this merged soul will start to move through his four bodies. The energy will partially move through different wiring than is normally used, and probably some subtle or clearly unfamiliar sensations will be the result. When someone regularly participates in constellations as a representative, a subtle purification and restructuring of his energetic structure will automatically follow. Most often, the effects of regularly representing others will not even be recognized as actual direct results of changes in the four bodies. Someone may notice that his view on certain things change, that certain issues and events seem less, or more important than before. Painful memories that always brought up a lot of emotions become just memories, and no specific feelings will be attached to them. Or, old themes may come to the surface and ask for attention again; cobwebs are pushed out of the subtle bodies by the other soul's presence. In classical shamanic practice, representing others has developed into a spiritual path. A representative in a constellation only represents a certain person once, but imagine a shaman who merges again and again with the same individual spirit helper. This helper is most often an animal spirit. Gradually, over the years, as he dances and sings, merged with this one specific spirit, the shaman's four bodies are purified, restructured, and strengthened. In the next chapter, I will explore the nature and effect of traditional shamanic forms of dealing with helpers and representing the spirits in more detail.

Most of the time, someone who has represented another person will be affected only in minor ways, and will not suffer from effects that he or she could not deal with. From a shamanic point of view however, some special care may sometimes be needed, for example when someone who has died only recently has been represented, or when it concerns someone who died in shock, or as the result of violence, murder, or an accident. Once, I was leading a constellation in which a man represented a client's uncle who had died less than a year ago. As he was representing the deceased man, the representative had an uncontrollable painful itch in his side, which lasted even after the constellation was finished. The client related that his uncle had suffered from a disease that had made it necessary to install a stoma, an artificial exit of the bowels. The itch the representative felt was exactly on the spot where the plastic tube had punctured the uncle's skin. I suspected that the continuing itch was a sign that the representative was still connected to the uncle's soul after the constellation, and this was confirmed by the representative who described that he felt the client's uncle was still standing behind him somehow. I suggested that the representative go out of the room, find a place where he could be alone for a few minutes, and there speak to the dead uncle, asking him to leave and withdraw into the world of spirit. After this little ritual, the itch was gone for half an hour, but then it started again. The dead uncle was clearly visible to me now, standing next to the client. Apparently he had a hard time leaving. I now asked the client to perform a little ritual and address his uncle. I asked him to invite his uncle to visit him that night in his dreams, so that any messages the uncle felt were important could still be given. The representative, itching skin and all, at the same time repeated the little ritual he had done earlier, but now firmly telling the uncle that it was no use trying to merge with him; if anything needed to be said and done he had to enter the client's dream. Only then did the itch finally stop completely, and did not return. When a representative notices an unexpected sensation or reaction after a constellation, it does not however always mean that there is still a connection with another person. Most often it will only be an effect of the changes in the four bodies of the representative himself, an effect of the temporal merging with the other's soul.

The connection between the representative and the other soul should be broken straight after a constellation, but from a shamanic point of view, there are some exceptions to this rule. Occasionally a continuation of the connection will bring additional necessary healing to the one who has been represented. Sometimes shamans help people who died in violent and confusing circumstances by keeping the other – including all the terror and confusion – in their own soul. Advanced practitioners may even allow the victim's astral body to merge completely with their own astral body. For a new practitioner this is often an overwhelming experience that can prove to be too hard to handle. An advanced practitioner will however simply embrace the suffering soul completely, and then through his own emotional control, he will gradually soothe its pain and fear. In such rituals for the dead, the healer may first weep and shake, allowing the other to enter his own subtle bodies and soul deeply, and as a result, he will actually experience the complete effects of the trauma the soul has suffered. However, although he feels the pain and confusion, the shaman will not identify with it, and carefully tries to help the other by offering clear thoughts and feelings of peace and strength. He will silently repeat sentences to himself such as: "This pain is from the past, all that caused it has stopped now. Behind these tears is the pure strength of your soul. The soul is healthy and free, the suffering was only there when you lived, and now you are dead. You live in spirit now, the pain has ended." After some time, the other's soul will become receptive and start to sense what it is being offered, and will usually slowly accept it. When it has reached a reasonable peaceful state, the shaman takes the soul to a place in the spirit world where further healing can be found, and releases it or turns it over to his spirit helpers who will take further care of it. These kinds of practices are very demanding, and are closely related to the dynamics described in the chapter about taking on suffering on behalf of others. They are also similar to the dynamics that occur in constellations when representatives experience and express the effects of severe trauma, with an important difference though: a shaman both feels and guides the other soul; in constellations, the representatives experience the feelings while the guidance of the other soul is in the hands of the facilitator.

According to the shamanic traditions, a person who has merged with a traumatized soul needs to purify himself and has to find new strength. The shaman (or, in the case of a constellation, the representative) needs to get a strong sense of his own soul again, so he can fully return to his familiar identity. His four bodies must be released of the stress imposed on them, and may need rest or even some repair. Traditional steps that are taken after this kind of work are cleansing with the smoke of specific herbs, bathing in specially prepared herbal baths, but also eating and singing. For western shamanic practitioners or for people participating as representatives in constellations, reading an inspiring book, taking a walk, listening to good music, and taking a hot bath are good additional alternatives. After representing a person with a particularly intense emotional trauma, a representative may choose to refrain from representing someone else for some hours or even days, until he is totally grounded in himself again.

The client, the represented family members, and the representatives are affected by systemic work, but the same is true for the other people who are present during the constellations, the participants in the seminar. Usually, they are sitting in a circle, around the area where the constellations are set up. During the seminar, each participant will usually be asked several times to be a representative, but most participants spend the greater part of the time sitting around the constellations. During a constellation, there is an interaction between the representatives and the other participants: the process of the representatives touches the participants, while the intense engagement of the participants deepens the experience of the representatives. In this way, the participants are part of the unfolding dynamic of the constellation; they cry when representatives cry, and feel lightened and relieved when a good resolution has been found. Specially archaic movements like a meeting with death, acceptance of a heavy fate, expressing sincere gratitude for having been given life, or respectfully saying goodbye to a partner after a relationship has broken down will touch all participants in their hearts. Each constellation offers an opportunity for finding new insights, and helps the participants to accept the complexity of the human experience. Even a participant who has not had the chance to be a representative will return home a changed person.

13. Development of the Soul

In traditional shamanism, the spirits are represented in several ways. They are present in songs that contain their instructions and promises; they are present in the altars and ceremonial objects that are dedicated to them. The spirits are also present when the shamans represent them by standing in their place, dancing with the spirit's movements, singing their sounds. Shamans' ritual dances in which the spirits are presented are not just simple imitations of movements and sounds; they are actually based on the same principles that make family constellations possible. Both the dancing shaman and the representative in a constellation stand in the place of someone else, feeling the other's essence in their own soul, looking at their surroundings through the other's eyes. Representing the spirits is actually a spiritual path, a path that leads to purification and expansion of the soul.

The spirits can be divided into four groups, and each group is approached in a different way. First comes the creator in his pure form, a single field of power. Next in line stand the grandfathers and grandmothers of the spirit world, the immense powers of nature. Then there are the spirits that are more or less of an equal level as humans for example, the spirits of the dead and the animals. Finally, there are the smaller spirits of nature. Shamans relate differently to each specific group of spirits.

The first and greatest, literally the biggest of all the manifestations of spirit that are recognized, is the creator, God. He is the creator of the universe. He may have a name such as 'Great Spirit', possibly he may even have a face that can be depicted – but that is it. In shamanic practice, this primordial power is mostly left intact without much interpretation, because there is no way to actually communicate with a power of such immensity. God in his essential state is spiritually much too immense for us to grasp or understand, he is very far away from us. The creator spirit is addressed and mentioned in prayers, but he seldom has a practical function in a healing ritual, or in any other rituals. All power comes from him; that is a fact and it is acknowledged, but we cannot deal with the source of 'all power' directly. The only possible relationship to this aspect of creation is one of total but simple respect and awe. Mentioning the creator in each prayer as the source of all that exists, the shaman bows down to this presence and acknowledges that it is not up to a human to understand. This most pure and highest level of spirit, God as the creator, does not reach out to humans. The shamanic traditions in their turn are not usually interested in the efforts needed to make some kind of direct experience of this energy possible, like some of the eastern meditation traditions do, for the simple reason that in shamanism, spirituality should stay within human dimensions. It does happen that shamans of higher degrees occasionally get a glimpse of this power, but that is almost like a by-product of their developed spiritual state. Also, sometimes one of the very powerful spirits like the Peyote grandfather may take a shaman's soul to be consciously immersed by the Creator. However, it is never the creator spirit himself who reaches out to us of his own accord. He simply exists, mysteriously, unimaginable.

Firstly, there is the creator spirit; next we find the grandfathers and grandmothers of the spirit world. Their nature is still immense and unimaginable, but at least they embody specific, defined, and therefore limited powers. The grandfathers and grandmothers are not nearly as huge as the creator spirit. Depending on the tradition, they will for example be the sun, the moon, maybe the earth and sky. The greater powers of nature like the sea, thunder, and the whirlwind may also fall under this category. It is possible for a shaman to communicate with the grandfathers and grandmothers of spirit, but it is not without risk: their touch may kill as well as transform or heal. The traditions teach that the grandfathers and grandmothers respond to the prayers of people who are spiritually purified. After having noticed someone who is praying to them for help, they may transfer some of their power, accompanied by a certain specific ritual or song. Such a song or ritual will then be used by the shaman to call the grandfathers in during a healing ceremony, and activate the power that was given by them. In essence, we relate to the grandfathers and grandmothers in much the same way we related to our parents and grandparents when we were still small. In the presence of the grandfathers and grandmothers of the spirit world, we become like small, helpless children, unable to understand much and incapable of taking care of ourselves. The grandfathers and grandmothers are much older than humankind; in matters of spirit they are more pure and evolved than us. Shamans will try to communicate with these spirits principally to ask them for power, either for power that can be used to help people in need, or for power that can be used by the shaman himself; power to help him see and fulfil his life's purpose. People will undergo quite extreme rituals in order to receive the attention and blessings from the grandfathers and grandmothers. The vision quest is the best known type of ritual used for this purpose.

During a vision quest, people will fast for three or four days and nights, but powerful medicine men or shamans may take up substantially longer fasts – up to a week or even more. All this time, the quester stays awake and prays to the grandfathers and grandmothers. Some will do this naked, others will be clothed or just covered with a single blanket. Staying put in a small place in nature, without food or water, praying day and night, the vision quester becomes like a helpless child, crying out in suffering. The language of the prayers is essentially the language of a child relating to his parents: "Grandfathers, I am pitiful in your eyes and cannot live without your support. Give me strength to understand, grant me a power so I may live. Help me to understand, help me with a power so I will be strong. Without your power I cannot live, I would not have air to breathe. Powers, make me strong." Such rituals are very demanding. A period of four days and four nights is a very long time when you are alone, fasting and praying. People are confronted with their weaknesses, especially their fears and doubts, and they will have to conquer these in order to open up for the grandfathers and grandmothers.

The vision quest and other related rituals are used to become fearless when facing the greater spirits. Shamanic traditions know many variations on the basic theme of fasting and praying. Sometimes people will symbolically lie down in a shallow trench covered with a blanket; others will be buried deep in the earth for the duration of this ritual. Sometimes the pit can be meters deep, the hole covered with wooden planks and earth. Sometimes people climb up a tree. The most extreme variation I personally heard was described by a Lakota elder and medicine man who once spent nine days and nights without food and water in a closed off dark cave. His chest and back were pierced with the claws of an eagle, and all through the ritual he was hanging in the air, dangling from ropes which were connected to these claws. It is not up to me to describe the meeting he had with the grandfathers during this time, but the grandfathers responded to his prayers, they did come to see him to show him a power. Such extremes are only chosen by experienced shamans and medicine people though; other people will just perform this ritual for a few days, sitting in nature – which usually is intense enough. Such rituals are especially extreme for medicine men, because only in extreme suffering will the human personality open up really wide for the power of the spirits. The healing power of the spirit is so great, it can only be absorbed when the personality is totally out of its normal confinements and when the four bodies are forced out of their habitual patterns.

Sometimes, no rituals are needed to receive power from the grandfathers; occasionally they choose to approach someone on their own initiative. If this is the case, that particular person is somehow akin to the grandfather, their natures are alike in some way, and because of this compatibility, the spirit's power can be relatively easily absorbed, without the mind and soul having to be opened up by many days and nights of praying and suffering.

There is a next group of spirits, which is more or less on an equal basis with humans, or at least they are close enough for us to speak with them relatively easy. Spirits belonging to this group are for example, the animal spirits, spirits of individual hills and rivers, and also the spirits or souls of the dead. Their world and our world are relatively close, spiritually seen we are neighbors. We have to find a balance with them like we have with the actual neighbors we have living next door in the physical world; we try to have a simple and workable communication, and when necessary, we will negotiate with them. Both spirits and humans benefit from a good relationship because gifts and information are exchanged. The spirits are given an altar and offerings of food, smoke, water, and songs, and in their turn they will help the shaman during healing ceremonies and give helpful information. Since they are more or less on an equal level with us, they see the world much in the same way as we do, which makes communication relatively easy. These are the spirits that are most important in shamanic healing rituals, since they can offer direct and practical help. A shaman who has learned how to reach them can communicate with them at almost any time he wants. Most of the spirit helpers of the shaman come from this level of spirits, and a shaman forms real bonds and friendships with them. However, they are spirits, and as such continue to be mysterious and powerful, and it is considered dangerous for the uninitiated to deal with them.

In my own shamanic work, I am helped by various spirit helpers. The bear spirit is one of them, one of the most powerful spirits of the category of spirits that is close to humans. It sought me out of its own accord by showing itself to me repeatedly in dreams, giving a series of teachings and instructions on how I could attune myself to it. For many years now, I have been undergoing a continuing purification and restructuring of the four bodies, just by regularly representing this spirit in healing rituals and dances. This restructuring happens on all levels; even my physical body undergoes subtle changes as a result of such contact with the bear spirit. It is not that I have become more hairy, or that my nails have turned into claws, I am still the same as I was before. But by allowing the bear spirit to use my voice, I can now make the grunts and sounds a bear makes. Also, I can sometimes look with the eyes of the bear spirit. Dancing to invite and to represent the bear spirit, after it has arrived and I am merged with it, I will see the skeletons of people right through their flesh. It is not a question of guessing: in a trance, merged with the bear, I can see the skeleton in the most literal sense, and can tell which bones have been broken or damaged, and if they have healed properly or not. When I started to be able to see these things, I did a series of tests because I wanted to be sure that what I saw was true. A few times, as I was teaching in a group, I asked about twenty volunteers to stand in a circle. Next I called in the bear spirit, dancing around the circle. Merged with the spirit, representing it, I would look at the bones of the people present and told them what I saw. I soon stopped these tests; participants in these experiments told me that my observations were correct. The gradual purification and restructuring of my four bodies by the bear spirit has continued over the years until this day. Merged with this powerful healer, I have been able to heal various types of trauma of the bone. Or more accurately: the bear did the actual healing work and I was only the helper that created and maintained the context of the healing ritual. I started doing actual healing work together with the bear about five or six years ago, and I have kept track of some of the clients I helped in the beginning to see if the healing was permanent or not; they are still free of pain and continue to have the freedom of movement they had gained after the bear worked with them. Strange or unbelievable as all this may seem for people who are unfamiliar with the shamanic traditions, my experiences with the bear spirit are not at all unusual or exceptional. There are many experienced shamanic practitioners who can share such stories as these. It might be good to mention here that although the communication with a spirit like the bear is relatively easy, it is never possible to predict how the spirit will behave. When I am lecturing somewhere, I always sing a few minutes for the bear spirit at the start and at the end of my talk. It regularly happens that a few days after a talk, I get a call from someone who was present in the audience who wants to tell me for example that during my song, they felt one of their vertebras click into a new position, and that a chronic pain has been gone since then. On the other hand, it also happens that during a healing ritual, the bear leaves almost immediately after coming in, obviously not able or not willing to help the client that asked for the ritual.

Finally, after the spirits that are close to us, there are also the smaller or lesser spirits. In communication with them the shamans must exercise some form of control. The relationship with the smaller spirits resembles the way we treat intelligent children. From this group, the small spirits of nature are best known because they lead an almost physical type of existence. Various cultures describe such spirits as goblins, trolls, elves, and so on. They are present in all natural environments, also in bigger parks, but they are seldom seen in the city. They sometimes act as gentle healing spirits or serve as messengers for the spirits of higher levels. Some spirits of this lower level can also be recruited to act as bad spirits, and then they are able to cause trouble. According to the various traditions, the small spirits have to be kept pacified by the shaman through regular gifts and offerings. The smaller spirits are usually not interested in us;

they will typically only seek our attention after we have disturbed them, to let us know we have to change our ways.

The word 'spirit' is used for all these different powers, from the highest to the smallest. All are recognized as manifestations of a single mystery, conscious aspects of creation. The shamans and medicine people I have met often say 'Spirit tells me', instead of 'This particular spirit tells me'. They will say 'Spirit is here' instead of 'The spirits are here'. The word spirit usually indicates both an individual spirit and the whole unspecified field of creation at the same time. Seen from a certain perspective, divisions between various types of spirit are not truly relevant, and the difference between them is superficial. Compared to the difference between spirits and humans, the differences between the various spirits themselves are not that big. Spirits can be big or small, but they are all living in the same subtle worlds, and do not have a physical body like us. Still, during shamanic training the apprentice must learn how to differentiate and relate to each group of spirits. With some, you are in a state of surrender and awe, with others, you negotiate, and with others, you stay on guard and in control. In shamanic practice, all these different types of relationships are included in the dealings with the mystery of life, and all are appropriate when used in the right context, so all need to be mastered.

The different ways of relating to spiritual powers in the form of spirits form the steps of a process of spiritual maturation. You start out feeling big and powerful, and with each step of the training you diminish further in size. The first step corresponds to being able to deal constructively with powers that are smaller than you are. You treat them with respect, but maintain awareness of your own will as you communicate with them. The next step is seeing that the other has equal value and shares capacities of the same nature as you yourself. The spirits then become your peers; you stop ordering them around and start to negotiate with them. You learn to work together, seeing that each of you will benefit when you are working as a team. You have shrunk in size: you are not bigger than the spirits anymore, instead you are the same size. The following step is the relationship with the grandfathers and grandmothers of spirit, the powers that are truly bigger than humans. To have a good relationship with them, you shrink further in size by continuous purification. Unless you purify yourself of opinions, ideas, and emotions, these will continue to fill you up so much that there will be no space left for the greater powers of the spirit. This phase is hard, since for example, all hidden feelings of superiority and inferiority must come to light and need to be dealt with. In order to relate in trust to powers so much greater than yourself, you have to have the courage to become very small again. Then, finally, when you are able to relax in the presence of the greater powers and let them guide you, you can move on to the next step. In this last phase, you shrink so much that you stop seeing yourself as separate from creation, only the creator spirit is left in your awareness. If a shaman is able to reach this point, it does not matter anymore if he speaks from his own mind or communicates with the spirit; he has become so pure there is no significant difference anymore. He is simply at ease with himself, and the boundaries between himself and creation are at the same time dissolved and still there. There are only a few shamans and medicine people who have been able to purify themselves and shrink in size until their soul expanded so much it could hold the creative force of life itself. The few who reach this purified state are considered holy people. They are recognized as the ethic leaders of their community; their help is sought by many, and their life and prayers serve as a continuous example for all.

The four steps of the shamanic path are not always easy to distinguish from one another. For practically all of the practitioners the shamanic training never stops, and the student continuously tries to master aspects of all steps simultaneously. He may work on exercising control over lesser powers and spirits while he is also learning to humble himself facing the grandfathers. Many traditional shamans and medicine people have started their training because as children they were able to see the spirits of the dead, and so they necessarily have to learn to deal with the spirits of this category first before they are taught to communicate with others. But no matter what the order of the steps is, they all have to be taken in order to get access to the full spiritual potential of the shamanic path.

Relating to the spirits opens the four bodies up so they can contain more and more power of the soul. And as the four bodies become less dense and less rigid, they will be able to be filled not only by the small personal soul, but gradually also by the greater soul. As a shamanic practitioner merges again and again with his spirit helpers, representing them in dances and rituals, such a gradual purification and restructuring is unavoidable. His four bodies open up for greater and stronger energy patterns, and as these patterns are imprinted, old patterns are pushed out and released. Some time ago, I had an experience that illustrates clearly how the spirit's presence purifies. I had been teaching in a festival in Holland, leading twelve workshops of two hours over a period of three days. At the end of each workshop I put my bearskin, which comes from Siberia, on the ground, and performed a simple ritual in front of it, making contact with my bear helper. During my dance I prayed and sang for the people who were present, and gradually merged with the spirit of the bear. Normally I only work this intensely with the bear spirit just once, and then take at least a few hours to recover. After dancing like this even just once, I need time to integrate the effect on my subtle bodies. During the festival I worked for more than ten times in a row, without time to fully recharge because I had to teach all the time. For a few days after teaching and dancing at the festival, I was very restless and felt like moving all the time. I had trouble going to bed, as soon as I lay down I wanted to get up again, and wandered through the house without aim, agitated and stressed. After five days of this I got to the point where I could hardly even sit down to eat anymore. At that point, my partner asked me some questions about what I felt exactly. Were the sensations I felt hot, cold, electric? Did they move through my body or were they static? Could I trace where my restlessness came from, where it was centered exactly? These questions made me realize that the restless feelings were located in my upper arms. Trying to move my arms in such a way that they would express exactly what I felt, I held my upper arms tight to my body, rigid and very tense, and moved my lower arms as fast as possible in all directions, as if I was helplessly trying to push myself away from something behind me. Soon I experienced utter exhaustion and a sense of deadening all over my body. Allowing myself to sit like this for a minute, weakly waving my underarms around, an image of the hospital came to my mind. That made me remember that as a one year old child I had been in the hospital for some months. I was seriously ill and finally nearly died of complicated infections. Remembering stories about my stay in the hospital, I jumped up and called my mother to ask her if I had been strapped to the bed during that time. My mother confirmed this. When I asked her how they did this, she told me I was only bound to the bed by my upper arms. I understood what had caused the restlessness of the last days and why I did not want to lie down in bed at night. The effect of my continuous bear dances had allowed a merging with the bear's spirit that was deeper than usual, and the strength of the spirit had obviously released some old cobwebs in the corners of my energetic and physical structure. The result was a release of a physical imprint of my very early childhood. Now knowing what the exact cause of my restlessness was, I simply allowed myself to feel it, and then breathed deeply, consciously moved my arms and body, telling myself I was free now and did not need to continue to struggle to be released from straps. For an hour or two my restlessness still increased, but after focusing repeatedly on the feeling of strength in my arms I have as a grown up man, my body slowly started to relax. The restlessness reduced, and after a day or so it was gone.

Through the practice of rituals and dances, shamanism offers a clear and structured path, a specific type of spiritual development. The result of the shamanic training is a slow and gradual expansion of the soul, or better said: increased space for the soul within the four bodies. This development is not often recognized as a true spiritual path since its methods differ from many other and better known spiritual schools and religions. Shamanic training is a bit odd compared to them. The yogi will try to calm down the 'inner fire' of his own passions and emotions, while the shaman will try to learn to exercise control over actual fire. The yogi will try to control his inner demons, while the shaman will speak with the spirit around him. The shaman does not practice meditation or use other techniques to reach a state of complete inner silence. On the contrary, instead of being silent, he does not stop talking. Advanced shamanic practice is a continuous improvised prayer that never stops, an ongoing dialogue with the natural and spiritual environment. And just as it takes years to become adept in meditation, it takes many years to learn how to pray in such a way that it leads to true spiritual maturity.

In a small and modest way, participating in family constellations can also be a path of purification and spiritual maturation. The representative who opens his soul for others purifies and restructures his four bodies, and this lets both the soul and personality expand. Regularly participating as a representative in constellations opens us up for 'the human experience' in all of its many aspects. A childless man can represent a father of seven children, and something in him will be changed by it. A healthy woman who has never been ill will look at herself differently after representing several handicapped people who lived with continuous physical pain and discomfort. The different steps of shamanic training can also be recognized in the constellations. In some cases, a representative bows down deeply for forces that influence his fate, for example for historic forces that are much greater than the individual. At other times, a representative has to be in full control of his life and act as a fully responsible individual, standing steadfast on the earth, saying no to certain forces of developments. And, most of the time, the representatives face each other and let go of differences, acknowledge each other as total equals, each having the right to belong, participating in both life and death. Although representing others in constellations differs from representing the spirits in traditional shamanic dances, still, being a representative makes us greater somehow; we become more connected, understanding and appreciative of humanity. When representing others is done with awareness, we gradually become greater than just our limited selves.

14. Some Pitfalls

Shamanism and systemic work have a lot of healing potential, but both have many specific pitfalls too. The two disciplines can be used and abused in many ways. There are some specific challenges that both the shamanic practitioner and the facilitator of systemic work face: both have to make sure they only offer a ritual or constellation when the client truly wants healing, and they have to be aware that their work can heal but also wound the soul.

In shamanic ritual and also in constellations, the source of information is mysterious. Even if it is understood that in shamanism, the spirits give information and in a constellation, the soul of a representative is able to experience sensations known to another soul, this understanding does not take away the mystery of the process. Some people feel that whatever comes out of a mystery should be left untouched, it should not be questioned. Although respect for the spirit and the soul are obviously essential in both shamanic practice and systemic work, this respect should not turn into blind obedience. In shamanic practice, blind trust eventually leads to dependency: someone may feel that the spirits are much more wise and powerful than himself, and spiritual; for someone like that the spirit's help is considered essential whenever a challenge arises. Asking information from the spirits can easily become compulsive, and then someone's own will and capacity to judge will gradually weaken. A similar thing happens with people who become involved in systemic work in a compulsive way. Whenever there is a question about work or family, they feel the need to set up a constellation so that information can be obtained and a strategy can be chosen.

The use of constellations to 'find out' about the present or the past can easily lead to serious distortions. Imagine that someone has been in therapy and found 'retrieved' memories of incest, but somehow he continues to doubt whether he was truly sexually abused in childhood. Now he wants to set up a constellation to find out if the memories are true. He will explain his case to the facilitator, and the audience is a witness to this conversation. When the facilitator agrees to set up a constellation in order to find out what has happened in the past, the people asked to represent the various family members are not free anymore. They know that whatever they will feel and experience during the constellation will determine whether the answer is 'yes' or 'no', which is quite a responsibility. When the representatives are set up in a situation like that, they are consciously or unconsciously under pressure, and they may sense some discomfort. The discomfort may be caused by the pressure that is the result of the context in which the constellation is set up, and probably does not originate from the soul of the people they represent. Still, that uncomfortable pressure may convince the representatives that something uncomfortable was going on in the past. However, even if the discomfort is truly coming from the other soul, that soul itself holds no true memories, no stories, no anecdotes. The soul just contains effects, imprints, and structures that are the results of experiences, not the experiences themselves. The soul looks at the world from the here and now, it does not dwell on the past. In a constellation, a representative can feel love, hate, or fear for someone else, but they cannot know why he feels this. The information about what exactly happened in the past cannot be found in the soul itself, only in the astral body and personality of the one who is being represented, and even then in a distorted form. Some things can be deduced from the body language of representatives, and from the ways they interact with each other, but that should never lead to definite conclusions about the detailed events that happened in true life. Setting up a constellation where all participants know that a certain question such as a history of incest is going to be checked will turn the constellation into a projection screen. Instead of freely experiencing what is felt, now everything is seen in the light of a certain question, and conclusions may be drawn that are absolutely inappropriate. I have seen some constellations that were set up by clients who wanted to find out things in the past, not just about incest but also questions like whether someone's father was his actual biological father or not, or if a client's parents had or had not been collaborators during the war. Often, when a constellation is set up in such circumstances, the responses of the representatives are confused and muddled. This is logical, since the souls of the ones who are represented may not want to be drawn in and will keep a distance. The representatives cannot sense the other souls so clearly, and as a result they will start to pay attention to their own unconscious responses to the question that was asked by the client. Gradually, as the representatives attune more and more to their own impulses, the signals from the other souls are lost. Shamanic practitioners are also regularly asked to clarify and determine whether certain things are true or not, whether certain choices are the right choice or the wrong one ... According to my personal ethics, a shamanic practitioner should never give answers to such questions. Instead of telling someone to leave his partner or stay, to buy this house or that, or to take a certain job while refusing the other, help should be given that enables someone to make their own choice with more strength and awareness. There are questions that can only be answered by the person who asks the question, and not by a shamanic practitioner or by a facilitator of family constellations.

Just as a facilitator of constellations must do, a shamanic practitioner also has to consider very carefully whether he will accept a client or not. One factor that he will look into is the client's motivation. Does someone want true healing, or does he simply want some obstacles removed without truly respecting the spirits and his own soul? If the spirits have been asked for support, and they have offered information and healing, the spirits will feel abused if the client thoughtlessly discards what is given. The offence they feel will usually not be expressed to the client, but to the shaman or medicine man who has asked them to help that particular client. If a shaman regularly asks the spirits to help clients who do not take the healing in, the spirits will sooner or later stop responding to his calls. A client can only accept healing power if he enters the ceremony with an open mind and heart, and with at least the willingness to accept other solutions than the ones he himself has already made up in his own fantasy. That is why preparing a traditional shamanic healing ritual takes a lot of time and effort; the shaman has to make sure that a client is truly determined to get well, otherwise his relationship with the spirits will gradually turn sour.

A facilitator who leads constellations also has to carefully observe the clients who ask to set up a constellation, and determine what it is they want. Do they ask for healing, or are they only asking that their difficulties be removed? Do they have the strength or courage to face what the greater soul will show them, and take it in? These are important questions. If someone wants to set up a constellation in order to determine whether he has been sexually abused in childhood or not, he is not usually asking for healing, he wants his doubts solved. If someone wants to use a constellation to find out whether his father is his biological father or not, he may want to know what type of respect he owes to the other, or he is possibly looking for a justification to judge or reject his parents. If someone wants to know whether his parents were collaborators during the war, he is not asking for healing for himself or for them, but is probably looking for some kind of permission to maintain his superior distant behavior towards them. The answers to such questions may be important to the personality and be relevant in the context of certain psychotherapeutic processes, but probing into these matters through constellations, or shamanic ritual, does not usually help the soul to heal. The souls and spirits of a certain family may only be invited with respect; they cannot simply be called to justice by people who feel superior to them.

The soul is powerful and it is also very fragile; it can be healed as well as wounded. Both the shamanic practitioner and facilitator of constellations create possibilities for the soul to take a step forward and express itself. When a soul or spirit is present in a shamanic ceremony, it is anchored in a temporary body. When it is thus anchored, it can be healed but it can also be attacked, and when that happens, the soul may get disoriented and is rendered powerless. In traditional shamanism, this principle is sometimes consciously used to make people ill: a shaman who wants to hurt somebody will create a vehicle for the intended victim's soul, and call that soul in. When the soul responds to the invitation and has come in, it will suddenly be violently attacked. The well known image of a witch doctor sticking pins in a little voodoo doll demonstrates one type of ritual that is used in various traditions to attempt to harm someone else's soul.

I have not seen conscious attempts to damage a soul during systemic work yet, but a soul can get wounded unintentionally during a constellation. Once, I was representing a man who was killed in the Kristallnacht, some years before the Second World War. I stood in line with two or three other representatives; we represented the members of a Jewish family that were killed. In front of each one of us was a man representing someone who was guilty of participation in the murder. The man who stood in front of me was continually speaking to himself, but so softly that I was probably the only one who could hear him. "I was a soldier, I had no responsibility. I was just following orders, there was nothing I could or should have done. It was just as it was, such were the times." When I had been invited to represent the murdered man, I had opened myself widely for his soul. Standing there, merged with him, I felt very vulnerable. The man in front of me was still acting like an aggressor, (although he might have disagreed with me if I had confronted him with this) and there was no way I could deal with it. The defensive repetitive mumbling felt like a series of punches to me; the man's mumbled and angry excuses sounded like screams in my ears, and I became so weak I could not even speak or move anymore. The facilitator obviously did not pay too much attention to what was going on with the various individuals. As the others in my line gradually reached some kind of resolution, I continued to stand there frozen and disoriented, while the representative in front of me just continued to explain to himself that he was innocent and had nothing to do with me whatsoever. Finally, the constellation was brought to an end, and the individual representatives were not asked any questions. I was pale, sick to my stomach and almost had to vomit, and I was like that for some hours. Seen from a shamanic perspective, the soul received a serious blow, and was literally traumatized by the constellation. I purposely say 'the soul' instead of 'my soul' or 'the Jewish man's soul'. When, during a constellation, a representative feels wounded, it is hard to differentiate between the two different aspects of the greater soul; in fact both my own soul and the murdered man's soul were violated. Any representative with a similar wounding experience will feel bad afterwards, and will most likely try to get rid of his bad feeling as soon as possible by trying to disconnect from the other's soul. However, when that happens, the other's soul will then be even more lost than it was before the constellation was set up.

If a facilitator is not able to recognize that a certain soul is disoriented or wounded after a constellation, he will not be able to offer a healing movement, and both the representative and the represented will suffer for some time. In the last parts of chapter ten, *The presence of the dead*, and chapter twelve, *The effects of constellations*, I described some shamanic ways that can be used to support a troubled soul; methods that could also be applied by someone who has represented a soul that has been wounded during a constellation. In the personal experience I have just described, the soul of the man I represented was wounded because of the way another representative acted. It is true that in systemic work a soldier who kills another soldier in wartime is not considered a murderer. But the man in front of me had not represented a soldier in wartime at all, he was simply a man who had voluntarily participated in the murder of Jews during peacetime, therefore he was a true murderer. The representative however had turned general observations made during systemic work into a dogmatic rule that he applied in the wrong context. In that way the constellation lost healing power – at least for me as a representative and the soul I represented.

Understanding the laws that govern systemic entanglements is essential for a facilitator and it can help representatives too, but it can obviously also become a pitfall. Feelings, body language and remarks of representatives may be interpreted too soon. Ideas and dogmas may overrule actual felt experiences. It should be taken into account that the client, audience, and representatives are all in a light trance, as I described in the chapter on timelessness. Whatever a facilitator says will have an immediate effect on how representatives interpret their own experience. The vast majority of the people who participate in a constellation will unconsciously try to accommodate the facilitator and will follow his consciously or unconsciously given guidelines. Therefore it is best to take time to allow the representatives time to feel and describe what their exact sensations are instead of rushing to conclusions.

Both shamanic and systemic work offer possibilities for the healing of the soul, and it is up to the practitioner and facilitator to make good use of these. Methods can be used and they can be abused – consciously and unconsciously. A skilful and respectful facilitator will be able to use systemic work as an impressive and effective healing method, but another will leave his clients frustrated or confused. Shamanic rituals can be inspiring and strengthening, but they can also be used in a stupid and demeaning way. I guess that only by truly opening up for the strength and vulnerability of your own soul will it be possible to find the strength, courage, and sensitivity that are needed to become a supporting witness to the healing of other's souls. Mistakes can and will still be made, and maybe they should occur every now and then, serving to remind us that we should not aim for perfection. When the shaman's and facilitator's own souls shine with clarity, the work they do will have a simple and natural beauty and power, and there will be little chance of abusive situations.

15. Rituals

Over the years I have used many healing rituals in my work. Most of these have been given to me by the spirits in dreams and when I was in trance. Some of the rituals address specific problems and questions, others help to bring balance in more general patterns and structures. Some rituals I have been using are based on the principle of representation as it is used in family constellations, or they are otherwise compatible with systemic work. In this chapter, I present a selection of rituals that may be helpful for the readers of this book, either for themselves or for their clients or groups. The descriptions I give focus on the organization of the space and the movements people can make in it. Reading these instructions, one may see these works as exercises. However, I call them rituals for a reason: When I do this type of work with the participants in my seminars, all the movements are accompanied by continuous drumming and lengthy improvised prayer songs. Prayers and invocations are said by all the people before, during, and after the actual movements, which, in combination with the drumming and singing, creates a light trance and helps people tune into the weight and purpose of the work. To me, the word exercise brings up associations with something of less depth. Rituals such as the ones I give here should not be used as substitutes for psychotherapy, family constellations, or other interventions by trained and professional therapists or trainers. I see the following rituals as supplementary healing practices that will help to create positive imprints on the soul, the four bodies, and the personality, and when used with understanding and respect, they can strengthen the effect of systemic therapy.

LET TRANS-GENERATIONAL ILLNESS FLOW BACK TO ITS SOURCE

If you are suffering from a problem or illness that runs in your family, trace the line back as far as you can. Maybe you know or find out that not only your father, but also your grandfather or even great-grandfather suffered from the same problem. Now visualize yourself, your father, grandfather and possible others who shared the same fate concerning this particular illness or problem. You visualize yourself in front, then your parent behind you, his parent behind him etc. At the end of this ancestral line, visualize the source of the disease, what has caused it. This may be a genetic defect, it may be an entanglement, it may be some specific emotional pain of suffering, an accident. You do not need to know why the chain started, just visualize the source of it as a field, a substance at the end of the line of ancestors. Now stand in front of yourself, facing the other you that you have visualized. You need a small bowl that you filled with water in which you dissolved some salt. Hold the bowl with salty water in your hands. Speak to the visualized version of yourself, and say something like: "The disease you carry is at least partially caused by reasons that originate in other people's lives. The energy you carry is not all your own. You can let go of that part."

Then, visualize that the aspect of the disease that does not come from your own life is absorbed by the salt in the water. Imagine that your visualized self becomes transparent now, and see all the trans-generational energy that causes your disease flowing into the bowl of water. Then let the image of yourself dissolve, step forwards to face your father. Follow the same procedure: ask him to let go of

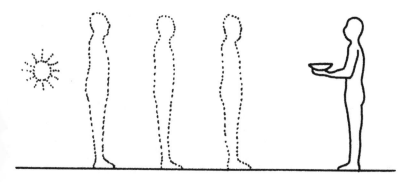

the trans-generational patterns and energy that have caused his disease, and then visualize that that energy flows into your bowl of salt water. Let his image dissolve and step forward so you face your grandfather. Repeat the same steps until you have reached the end of the line, and all the visualized images of your ancestors are gone: now you are face to face with the field or the energy that lies at the roots of the disease in your family. Now say something like: "This is where the disease in my family belongs, now all of that returns to its source." If it feels natural to you, you can pray for health and help and healing for yourself, and all the family members who have suffered or still suffer from the same disease or trouble. Now put the bowl of water on the ground, and leave it there as you take a step backwards. Now visualize the ancestor who stood closest to the origin of the disease, maybe it was your grandfather or great-grandfather. Visualize him now without the disease, free and happy. Send some good thoughts to him. You may want to present yourself to your ancestor, and tell him about your life, what is good about it, what you are proud of. In this way, the ancestors can use their joy about your life to fill up the hole that was created when the disease was leaving them. They will feel strength and happiness because life continues well. Then, take another step back, call back the image of the ancestor who stood second in line, visualize him happy and well and greet him. Repeat the steps until you are facing a visualized version of yourself again, and tell yourself too about the good things in your life. Then you can turn around, step in the image of yourself and merge with it. The ritual is finished. Leave the bowl with salt water in its place for one or two days before flushing the contents down the toilet.

FINDING STRENGTH THROUGH ANCESTORS IN CASE OF TRANS-GENERATIONAL ILLNESS

Visualize yourself and the members of earlier generations in your family who had the same disease as you have, especially those who were strong and lived reasonably happy lives. See them standing in a line behind you, looking forward to the beginning of the line where your visualized self is standing. Then invite or visualize the sources that gave them the strength to carry their fate and cope with their difficulties. Visualize these powers in any form that feels natural to

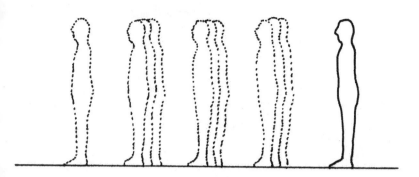

you; you could imagine angels standing at your ancestor's sides, but also animals or abstract forces. Stand at the back of the line, next to the ancestor that was born most long ago. Greet your ancestor, and tell him that you suffer from the same disease as he, and inform him that you have come looking for support. Then make contact with the sources of strength that supported this ancestor, and ask them to support you to. Allow yourself time to really feel and absorb what these sources of strength have to give to you. Then, give thanks and take a step forwards. Repeat the same step as you stand next to the second ancestor, and when ready, step forward again, until you end up standing next to your own position. Step into the position of your visualized self and feel all the ancestors behind you, and feel their connections to sources of strength. Then make a connection to the sources of strength that have supported you until now in your life, and allow the sources of strength of your ancestors to merge with them. In this way, you join with your ancestors on the level of strength and dignity, instead of the level of disease. You can stand in line with them, accepting strength from those who can give it, so you will have additional strength to accept what life has given you. Standing there, with a silent strength, connecting your own sources of strength with those of your ancestors, you receive something good, but you also give something to those behind you. You, in your turn, give strength to your ancestors and add dignity to their life.

Finding Strength after Sudden Irreversible Change in Life

It is not only possible to connect to sources of strength of members of earlier generations within your own family, the previous ritual can also be done to connect to sources of strength that supported those who share the same fate as you. Imagine you have been diagnosed with a serious and threatening illness, and now you have to get certain radical treatments in the hospital. Or, you had an accident, and one of your limbs has been amputated; somebody you loved has been killed in a car crash. Even if you have no family members or ancestors who have had this experience, there are many people who had to face the same situation as you. Many of them have managed to get back on track sooner or later. When you are confronted with a sudden and irreversible change in your life, you can perform a variation of the former ritual. Instead of family members, visualize a number of people who have suffered the same thing as you, who managed to find strength in the good things their life still had to offer, who were able to start again somehow. Follow the same steps as in the ritual with family members: first introduce yourself to these people and then ask for contact with the sources of strength they have. Introduce yourself to these sources and make a connection to them. Maybe you are not yet able to visualize your own sources of strength and the merging of these with the strengths of the other people. You can always repeat the ritual at a later time and then finish this last step.

An Altar for the Family Soul

In a shamanic context, the ancestors are not just our parents, grandparents, and so on, but also those family members who died young and those who never had children. That is why traditional people often speak about 'the former generations' instead of the ancestors, including all who lived before and were part of the family in one way or another. In systemic work, many facilitators speak of the 'family soul', meaning a consciousness that also includes all the members of earlier generations in the family. This family soul is an active force that influences our lives. What was good in the lives of earlier generations becomes strength that flows to us; what was unresolved becomes manifest as disturbance. The individuals who are included in the family soul are present in our lives; they both bless and trouble us. The spiritual power of a shaman or medicine man who has died can, after his death, appear again in a next generation. According to traditional people I have met, the powers of the shamans and medicine people may reappear in direct descendants and family members who are born up to seven generations later. The same is true for all spiritual strength that people have developed in their lives; later generations may benefit from it. There is a simple ritual that can be done in order to receive some of the strength, skills, and powers that can come to us via the family soul: the construction of an ancestor altar or family soul altar.

Such an altar does not need to be a complicated and elaborate structure. Start by choosing a spot in your house that will be relatively undisturbed, for example an empty space on a bookshelf or on a small cupboard. Essentially, the altar is simply made from small objects that belonged to or represent family members of earlier generations. It may include photographs, rings or jewelery, personal belongings, and symbols. Your parents, grandparents, and those family members with whom you have a specific connection, or whose lives or fates have special meaning for you, can each be individually represented by a single object or photo; other family members may be represented by general symbols. If, for example, the family of your mother originally came from Hungary, you can also add a little map of Hungary. When the altar is installed and it looks attractive to you, include a small candelabra and a cup. Now, for a certain period of time, you give the family soul a small white candle and some fresh water every day. You choose a period of time, for example a month, three months, half a year or even a year, and during that time, you continue to light a candle and pour a few drops of fresh water every day. If you go on a vacation or otherwise have to be away from home for some time, count the days you will be gone and before you leave light a candle for every day you will be gone. You can burn several candles at the same time; as you light each candle you mention which day it is for. Such an altar is used by the family soul to purify and strengthen itself. The good things that can come from the family soul can flow more easily; the entanglements that are the legacy of your family can be a bit easier to solve.

STRENGTHENING THE FLOW OF LIFE FORCE THROUGH THE GENERATIONS

This ritual can be done for somebody who is ill and needs strength in order to make a move towards healing. The person who needs help is given a place that can be occupied by himself or by a representative. From this place, two lines are drawn: one for the line of generations of the mother's family, the other for the father and his family.

Each line has seven steps; it goes back seven generations. Apart from the father and mother, you do not have to distinguish between individuals, just see the steps in the lines as steps into the general field of a certain generation. The first person placed in the space is the client, and with his parents two lines start. The next step is their parents, then their parents etc. To start the work, the leader of the ritual walks slowly through the different zones, and in each zone, invites that specific generation of ancestors for whom that place is reserved. After this, a woman stands in the line of the mother's family, on the place of those who are most far away in time from the client. At the same time, a man takes the position of the seventh generation on the father's line. In this place, the two representatives pray, and ask that the life force that created and supported this seventh generation be passed on from where they stand to the people of the next generation in the line. They are not tuning in to specific individuals, but ask support and blessings from a whole generation of ancestors for all the ones that will come after them. When the representatives feel the ancestors of the seventh zone supporting the flow of life towards the sixth generation, they can take one step forward. They do not have to move in the same tempo, it is best if they move individually. Standing in the place or zone of the sixth generation of ancestors, they repeat the same question or prayer. Standing there, they pray again for the flow of life and strength to flow forwards. When they sense that the flow is strong enough, they let it move them another step forwards to the next generation, and so on. Finally, the male representative is standing in the place of the client's father, the female representative in the place of the mother. There, together, at the same time, they let all the strength and power coming from the ancestors behind them flow forward to the client.

During the process of moving through the generations, the two representatives may sometimes experience strong emotions or even

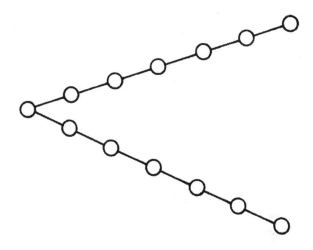

get stuck. When the energy that is encountered in the zone of a specific generation is very heavy or painful, a representative may take time to process the feelings there, but it can also happen that he starts to fight or resist the experience. When the representatives are fighting, they actually start to use the life force they are trying to carry forwards, and nothing will be left to give to the next generations. Fighting, the representatives will use the life force for themselves to gain strength to fight the obstruction. Such a fight is always the result of tuning into a specific individual's feelings and strategy in life. When I see someone getting stuck this way, I ask him to stop fighting, and encourage him to simply feel what there is to feel. After a few seconds, I ask him to visualize a symbol of strength in front of himself. Then I suggest that the representative steps through this symbol as if it were a door, into the next zone of ancestors, holding on to the line of life force he has been carrying forwards throughout the ritual.

STRENGTHENING THE FLOW OF GIVE AND TAKE

This ritual helps people to sense the ongoing flow of power through their lives, a power which is not theirs, which is greater than they are, but one they can use all the same.

A pattern of concentric circles is laid out on the floor, so that there are five circular zones. The middle zone of the ritual space represents the unknowable source of life. The circles indicate zones that are one by one further away from this power. This does not mean that the further zones are polluted or inpure; they are simply successively further away from the original source of life and strength. The participants start out in the middle circle, with their back towards the center. During the ritual, participants do not look or go there. The middle zone, where they stand, represents their own life. Behind them are zones where the people can be found that gave life, power, or teachings to the participants. The further backwards they go, the further the participants step back in time: first they find themselves in the zone of their parents, after that, in the space of their grandparents. The circle connected to the parents is also the place of the participant's teachers and spirit helpers; the circle of the grandparents is also the circle of the teachers' teachers and the helpers' helpers. In front of the participants there are two circles, reserved for the generations that will benefit from the participant's wisdom and creativity. The first circle is connected to those who will be raised and taught by the participants, the following circle stands for the people who will come after them.

Before the participants start to move back and forth through the circles, you take a moment to dedicate the ritual. You could pray out loud for the people there, asking that they will be able to find their place in the chain of life, find a way to participate fully in this timeless giving and taking. You can ask the helpers to support the ritual, so that something good will flow from the source of life to all participants, and that they will all know they have something to give to others. Then, participants can start moving through the different zones according to their own feeling. They can go fast or slow, they can first go forward or they can first go backward, they can go back and forth several times or just once. They step into the place of those who came before them, and of those who will come after them, always facing outwards from the center. After some time, usually after

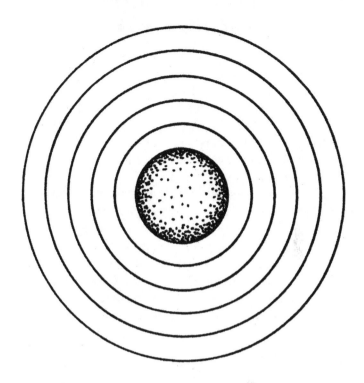

twenty minutes or half an hour, everybody naturally comes to rest again in the starting position, the third circle. Then you can end the ritual with a small prayer, for example by asking for blessings from the source of life; or you can visualize together that all will continue to feel the strength that was received and will be able to give some of it to those who need it.

Receiving Strength from an Unknown Ancestor

Of the various rituals I have developed to get access to ancestral strength, the following is the most simple. It can be done on your own, or with a group of people. The first step is to visualize the structure of a family tree, lying on the ground behind you. The successive generations of ancestors can be seen as steps backward in time. In this ritual, it is best to avoid visualizing individual ancestors behind you; otherwise you get confused easily. Instead, imagine a series of zones, each zone holding another generation of ancestors.

Then, with this image behind you, close your eyes and respectfully ask entry to this field. Ask specifically for contact with an ancestor that can give you strength; ask to be guided to an ancestor that will be able to support you. Then ask that this ancestor make itself known to you, and say that you will go looking for him or her during the ritual. You can ask for protection and guidance from your helpers or the powers that support you with your life and work as you descend through the lines of ancestors. Before you start moving, take some time to start sensing a specific benevolent ancestor behind you. When you have succeeded with this, slowly start stepping backwards. Take steps as your body directs you until you have reached the zone in which this ancestor stands. You may first step into the place of your father, second into that of your father's mother, then of her mother, then of her father, of his father etc. Most people feel a response from an ancestor anywhere from the fifth generation, and often as far as in the eight or ninth generation. Simply move backwards until you come to a stop at the place where you sense the presence of the ancestor that can support you and give you strength. Having arrived at the zone of this ancestor, stand still, sit, or lie down as feels right to you. Simply open up for his or her blessing. You may sense some specific movement or flow of energy, or even see or hear the ancestor while you have your eyes closed. If you have been trained in shamanic techniques, you can enter a light shamanic trance before starting to walk backwards, and at this point, you can communicate consciously with the ancestor and ask for blessings. After some time, you will feel it is enough, and then you can say goodbye. In parting, you can ask the ancestor if you may visit again. If you feel like it, you could also give the ancestor permission to appear in your dreams. Then you start to

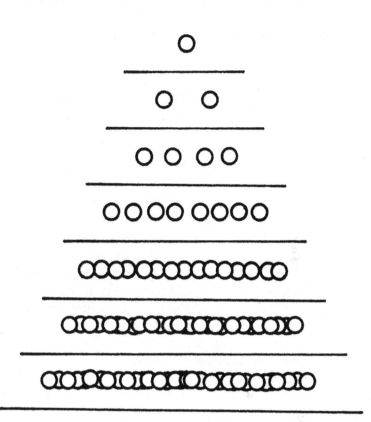

walk forwards again, leaving the ancestor in his or her own zone. Walk forwards consciously until you are back in your own life, in the starting position, and then open your eyes again.

STRENGTHENING THE FLOW FROM PAST TO FUTURE

This ritual can only be done by a group of people; a minimum of about twelve participants is needed. Divide the room into three zones: two big open spaces separated by a long strip of about a meter width in between. One wide zone represents the past, the dividing strip represents the present; the second wide zone represents the future. The participants start the ritual sitting in the middle zone, everybody looking to the future. When you are in the zone of the present, you are representing yourself, your own life, and you can sit there as often and as long as you like. You can also stand up and move backwards or forwards, but when you stand in the zone of the past or the future, you do not represent yourself anymore. In the zone of the future, you take a position facing someone who is still sitting in the zone of the present, and now you represent something good that is waiting for them in the future. When you stand in the zone of the past, you stand behind one of the people who sit in the zone of the present, and now you represent a strength from the past, which enables the one who sits in front of you to connect to the future. You represent something or someone good, and you do not need to know any details about what or who you represent. Standing in the past, you open yourself for something good out of the past from the person in front of you. Representing this strength, you let it flow forwards towards the other. It may be that you get an impulse to lay your hands on the back of the one sitting in the present, and this you can do – but do not move your hands while touching the other, just silently place them on the other's back and keep them still. When you have chosen to stand in the zone of the future, you may have your eyes closed or you can look into the eyes of an individual sitting in the zone of the present. You represent something good for him or her, something that may happen, some object that they will acquire or a good person that the other will meet. Standing in the zone of the future, you silently invite the other to come to you. Without words, feel your heart reaching out, welcoming the other. There may be moments when you feel you want to reach out and take the other's hands, and you can do this. Do not pull the other towards you into the future however, just stand still, welcoming the other in silence. During this ritual, you may also feel you have to stand behind someone in the past or future who is already representing

somebody or something, and a short chain of strength or a chain of inviting potential may be formed this way.

Even if there are people behind you giving you strength from the past, and people in front of you are inviting you, you stay where you are. Just sense the power behind you and absorb it, and let the invitation in front of you help you to expand your trust. Feel the strength of the past that moves through you and connect it to the future. Let all the energy in, but do not act on it, let the power simply build up so the connection between good things in the past and in the future gets stronger and stronger. When it starts to feel like it will be too much, or when it simply feels right, you stand up and move out of the present. You do not have to wait until the people in the past and future have moved away from you; you can stand up at any time. The people who were in front of you and behind you will simply move to another position. Always remember one important restriction during this ritual: when you sit in the here and now you may not move forwards as yourself. In the zone of the past or the zone of the future, you take a position as a representative for good things for somebody else. During the ritual, the participants move slowly and in silence through the zones. Everybody spends time in all three zones – moving here and there just as they sense it is right. The ritual usually comes to a natural close after about half an hour or so, when everybody retreats back into the here and now, facing the future.

About the Author

Daan van Kampenhout, born 1963, studied with traditional shamanic teachers from different cultures. However, the most important teachers have been and continue to be the spirits, who appear in his dreams and during ceremonies.

Since 1986 he has been teaching and lecturing internationally on the subject of shamanism. In 1993 he founded the Practice for Shamanism and Ritual. He is the author of three books and many articles about traditional and contemporary shamanic practices. Part of his work, both articles and books, has been translated from the Dutch and published in French and German.

Daan van Kampenhout conducts courses all over Europe on Shamanism and Family Constellations.

For more information please contact him at: dvk@xs4all.nl

Contact Address:
Daan van Kampenhout
Practice for Systemic Ritual
Postbox 10092
1001 EB Amsterdam
Netherlands